HAMILTON

OTHER BOOKS BY TONY WILLIAMS

Washington and Hamilton: The Alliance That Forged America (2015), with Stephen F. Knott

The Jamestown Experiment (2011)

America's Beginnings: The Dramatic Events That Shaped a Nation's Character (2010)

Pox and the Covenant: Franklin, Mather, and the Epidemic That Changed America's Destiny (2010)

Hurricane of Independence (2008)

HAMILTON

An American Biography

TONY WILLIAMS

ROWMAN & LITTLEFIELD
Lanham • Boulder • New York • London

Published by Rowman & Littlefield
A wholly owned subsidary of The Rowman & Littlefield Publishing Group, Inc.
4501 Forbes Boulevard, Suite 200, Lanham, Maryland 20706
www.rowman.com

Unit A, Whitacre Mews, 26-34 Stannary Street, London SE11 4AB

Distributed by NATIONAL BOOK NETWORK

British Library Cataloguing in Publication Information Available

Library of Congress Cataloging-in-Publication Data

Names: Williams, Tony, 1970– author.
Title: Hamilton : an American biography / Tony Williams.
Description: Lanham : Rowman & Littlefield, 2018. | Includes bibliographical
references and index.
Identifiers: LCCN 2017055275 (print) | LCCN 2017056132 (ebook) | ISBN
9781538100189 (Electronic) | ISBN 9781538100172 (cloth : alk. paper)
Subjects: LCSH: Hamilton, Alexander, 1757–1804. | Statesmen—United
States—Biography. | United States—Politics and government—1783–1809.
Classification: LCC E302.6.H2 (ebook) | LCC E302.6.H2 W734 2018 (print)
| DDC 973.4092 [B]—dc23
LC record available at https://lccn.loc.gov/2017055275

∞™ The paper used in this publication meets the minimum requirements of
American National Standard for Information Sciences—Permanence of Paper
for Printed Library Materials, ANSI/NISO Z39.48-1992.

Printed in the United States of America

214-6045

To Ray and Nancy Fahrmeier, with gratitude and love

CONTENTS

ACKNOWLEDGMENTS

I **want to** thank Jon Sisk and his team at Rowman & Littlefield for their great enthusiasm for this book and their excellent work publishing it. This is the second book we have done together, and I look forward to many more. Thanks to Jon for a memorable lunch that included great conversation and Maryland crab cakes during a visit.

It has been a great joy to write this book with the constant encouragement of so many family members and friends. David Bobb, Bruce Khula, Steve Knott, and Jeff Morrison have been pillars of friendship in my life and models of scholarship and character. Steve deserves a very special thank you for coauthoring *Washington and Hamilton: The Alliance That Forged America*, reading the manuscript for this book, and being a good friend. He is the best Hamilton scholar around. I also want to thank all of the following people for excellent conversations, scholarly collaboration, and friendship: Sam Agami, Paul Carrese, Jack and Tanya Cheney, Daniel Dreisbach, Josh Dunn, Hank Edmondson, John Ericson, David Gowdy, Dianna Greenwood, Rebeccah Heinrichs, Kirk Higgins, Mike and Jessica Hosang, Michelle Hubenschmidt, Amanda Hughes, Liz Kaufer-Busch, Sally Khula, Stuart Leibiger, Gordon Lloyd, John and Cheryl Lynch, Michael Maibach, Ken Masugi, Rob McDonald, Bob McKenna, Stacey Moses, Phil Munoz, Mackubin Owens, Julie Ponzi, Joe Postell, David Raney, Amanda Read, Alec Rogers, Kathy Saar, Garrett Ward Sheldon, Julie Silverbrook, Grace Struiksma, Jim Swords, Robert Van Ness, Art Ward, Gennie Westbrook, and all the families of Williamsburg Revolution and Venom baseball. A special thanks to all my colleagues—and all of our teachers—at the Bill of Rights Institute who are doing incredibly brilliant and important work advancing civics education across the country. I enjoy presenting several lectures at Colonial Williamsburg annually and really appreciate all the efforts of Trish Balderson to make them happen.

Finally, I want to thank my wife, Lynne, and our children, Catherine and Paul, for all of their support. This book was slightly delayed by attending all of their baseball, basketball, soccer, volleyball, crew, and spring track events, spending time as a family, going to the movies and taking hikes together, reading books at coffeehouses, going on family trips, watching the New York Yankees and Syracuse Orangemen, and generally doing the things that make life worth living.

This book is dedicated to my father-in-law, Raymond Fahrmeier, and my mother-in-law, Nancy Fahrmeier. Nancy tragically passed away on Easter Sunday while I was writing this book. They have been a great source of support through more than twenty-five years, and I am eternally grateful for the gift of their daughter and their love.

INTRODUCTION

Alexander Hamilton was an immigrant from the West Indies who became a quintessential American. From his arrival on the shores of his adopted country, he imbued American principles of liberty and self-government that shaped the American Revolution and laid the foundation of the country for more than two hundred years. Shedding his Caribbean heritage, he quickly identified himself as an American. His allegiances were not merely to the revolutionary Patriot cause, but to a broader love of country he embodied throughout his life.

As the colonies went to war with Great Britain, Hamilton enthusiastically went to war to prove his mettle and courage for his personal honor and fame. But he went to war for a larger purpose beyond himself and his own immortality. He joined the cause in the militia to defend American principles against British oppression. He unhesitatingly fought in the war and laid his life on the line because he held those principles as sacred as any native-born American subject of Great Britain.

Hamilton was an ambitious young man who thirsted for fame and glory. But his ambition was of a noble kind. It drove him frenetically throughout his life to serve the American republic in war as a hero and in peace as a lawgiver imitating the lives of the great Greeks and Romans. He selflessly and faithfully served the public in the highest echelon of leadership during the war, a legislator in the New York Assembly and the national Congress, a delegate to the important national and state conventions that led to the creation and ratification of the Constitution, and the treasury secretary.

The rising American republic he helped to create was the perfect vehicle for Hamilton's noble ambitions. Washington's leadership principles were rooted upon allowing a man to rise by his merit rather than aristocratic birth. Hamilton seized the opportunity and soon became one of the most trusted aides to the commander-in-chief. Demonstrating his administrative genius and talents in numerous ways during the war, Hamilton then entered politics and lent those talents to building the American regime. At first frustrated by the lack of national vision among many other politicians during the 1780s who frustrated his continental designs, the opportunity to serve in the cabinet as Washington's right-hand man allowed him to shape the American economy and constitutional order brilliantly.

As a foreigner with an internationalist economic perspective gained at a mercantile firm in the nexus of imperial trade in the West Indies, Hamilton was not bound by the localism that tied people to their colony or later their state. The Continental Army was especially significant as a unifying force especially for officers to think of themselves as Americans first. Throughout the 1780s, General Washington spoke often of the national Union, and Hamilton wrote many essays that showed he was thinking continentally. His statesmanship in the same decade was profoundly and uncompromisingly dedicated to the creation of a stronger constitutional government and national Union. As treasury secretary under President Washington, Hamilton consolidated the national American economy through his comprehensive financial program and linking the diverse parts of the economy together.

Hamilton's Americanism was deeply informed by the somewhat anachronistic eighteenth-century concept of honor. Honor was the measure of a man, the preservation of one's public reputation. To have honor was to be heroic and manly. An honorable man was free of debt and not dependent on any man. It was to have an unblemished, upstanding integrity and dignity. Federalist Fisher Ames thought that Hamilton was "inflexible" on every point of honor. Undoubtedly, Hamilton was gravely committed to the code of honor. Hamilton was involved in nearly a dozen challenges about honor that nearly led to duels even while serving in the army and as a statesman. Ultimately, the duel with Aaron Burr took Hamilton's life too early and negated any further contributions to the rising republic. Hamilton was just as serious about the national honor because its politics, economy, and national security were key ingredients in its reputation abroad and its very survival. His decades of public service were spent in crafting an honorable constitutional republic and capitalist economy.

For a man of humble—and some would have said dishonorable—origins, Hamilton doubly felt that he had to prove himself worthy among other American statesmen. This was especially true when his political opponents would not let him forget his difficult early impoverished circumstances and official illegitimacy. Nor would they let him forget he was an immigrant, a foreigner to the United States. Even though many important founders were born in other countries, Hamilton's enemies used it as a weapon to question his patriotism and loyalty to American principles. The charges were personally insulting and patently absurd for a war hero, congressman, author of the *Federalist*, and the first treasury secretary.

Not that Hamilton was merely a victim of vicious personal attacks. He brought on several problems himself. He seemed to have a bit of a chip on his shoulder, likely because of his lowly childhood, that made him prone to have a thin skin. He was at times arrogant due to his brilliance and dismissive of opposing views. While his judgment was usually good and his political strategic sense was often keen, his huge lapses sometimes surprised his contemporaries as much as they baffle us today. The disastrous public revelation of the sexual liaison with Maria Reynolds and his party infighting with John Adams were only two examples of exercising poor judgment. He placed himself in difficult personal challenges that robbed him of happiness and suffered dire political consequences for his political career building the republic.

Hamilton's tragic flaws make him all that much more interesting to study. American politicians during this period were rarely unified in their visions and policies. This was just as true in the Revolutionary War, Confederation period, and debate over the Constitution as it was during the notably partisan and vicious 1790s. The contentious Hamilton contributed a hefty portion of divisiveness to national councils.

Yet his political vision of national Union and his financial vision for a unified and dynamic economy helped bring the nation together constitutionally and economically in his key role as nation builder.

Alexander Hamilton has obviously been the subject of much recent popularity, even frenzied adoration. Lin-Manuel Miranda's Broadway play was a stroke of creative genius that has unleashed a wave of Hamilton-mania and popular interest in the history of the American Revolution and founding. The play helped to restore Hamilton to the pantheon of founding fathers in the popular imagination. Three excellent biographies of Hamilton stand out in a growing library of books dealing with the subject. Historian Forrest McDonald wrote the brilliant academic study *Alexander Hamilton: A Biography*, which remains a standard of scholarship forty years later. Biographer and historian Richard Brookhiser has penned numerous biographies of the founders, including the excellent *Alexander Hamilton, American*, which is a Plutarchian study of character as well as examination of his American continental outlook. Miranda's play was based upon the magisterial biography *Alexander Hamilton* by Ron Chernow, which has been devoured by Hamilton fans. There are numerous excellent books that study Hamilton's relationship with other founders, fine academic books on his political philosophy, or that examine his reputation in history. But if a curious person walks into a bookstore, chances are that their only option will be the massive Chernow tome that may frighten them away.

This biography seeks to place a brief, readable book into the hands of interested readers. It is consciously popular history aimed at a general audience who may have watched a few documentaries or read a couple of books on the founders and want to learn more about our nation's founding and its principles. Because it is a brief, popular biography, I have decided to modernize the quotations for readability and dispense with the customary scholarly convention of referencing the primary sources (which can be found in my *Washington and Hamilton: The Alliance That Forged America* for interested readers). *Alexander Hamilton: An American Biography* explores how its subject helped create the American experiment in liberty and self-government, and how his own life was in turn profoundly shaped by it.

CHAPTER 1

THE RISE FROM OBSCURITY

The West Indian islands where Alexander Hamilton was born and raised could hardly have been more different from the British colonies in North America. The Caribbean was the nexus of European imperial struggle because of the valuable commodity of sugar. The islands were a paradise for their great beauty and opportunities, which belied great problems and horrors. The sugar plantations and trade produced great inequalities of wealth with fortunes made by a favored few and grinding poverty for most. Europeans imported African slaves whose populations were ravaged by tropical diseases and horrid work routines on sugar plantations. Over the centuries, they died by the millions and were replaced by new slave imports. The attraction of easy wealth for planters attracted dreamers and fortune seekers.

Alexander Hamilton was born to humble origins in difficult circumstances on the Caribbean island of Nevis. Few would have predicted his meteoric rise considering the cards he was dealt. His mother, Rachel Lavien, lived a mostly marginal life, though her difficulties were not entirely of her own making. Rachel grew up in a broken home after her mother left her father. At only sixteen, she married John Lavien and bore a son, Peter. She was accused of engaging in adulterous affairs, which landed her in the dank confines of a Christiansted prison on St. Croix. When she was released, Rachel fled her abusive husband and moved to the island of Nevis. She quickly hooked up with dreamer and ne'er-do-well James Hamilton and had two sons by him out of wedlock. Alexander Hamilton was born in 1757 and declared an illegitimate bastard when John Lavien divorced Rachel for "giving herself up to whoring" and being "shameless, rude, and ungodly." Hamilton would suffer the stigma for all his life.

The challenges Hamilton and his family faced were about to go from bad to worse. James Hamilton moved his family to St. Croix in 1765 but promptly abandoned them. Rachel became a single mother struggling to eke out an existence for her two boys by running a small provisioning store and renting out her slaves. In February 1768, tragedy struck yet again when Rachel and Alexander suffered a tropical fever to which his mother succumbed. When she died, Alexander and his brother were now illegitimate orphans whose meager inheritance was unexpectedly claimed by John Lavien. To compound their misery, their guardian committed suicide. At that point, Hamilton had virtually no prospect of succeeding in life to the smallest degree. He was stuck on the extreme margins of West Indian society and presumably bound to a dismal fate.

Hamilton did not surrender to his circumstances, however, and made the most of small opportunities. He had not received much of an education but had inherited thirty-four books from his mother. This modest shelf of books contained several great books including the Bible, Plutarch, Machiavelli, and Alexander Pope. His reading taught him character lessons in virtue and honor.

Hamilton had the great fortune to apprentice as a clerk at the import-export firm Beekman & Cruger. His training included the essentials of international trade, accounting, currency exchange, and management. The opportunity allowed Hamilton to develop a knack for administration. Despite his youth, Hamilton was left in charge of the company for lengthy periods of time. He proved himself both precocious and presumptuous. He acted well beyond his age and station, bossing around ship captains and reprimanding them for the inferior quality of their cargoes. He fired the firm's attorney for negligence. Yet owner Nicholas Cruger strongly endorsed Hamilton's actions when he returned from business in New York.

For all of his talent and success, Hamilton hated being a clerk and dreamed of achieving greater things whatever the odds. He wrote a revealing letter to his friend, sharing his imaginings:

> [I] confess my weakness, Ned, my ambition is prevalent that I condemn the groveling and condition of a clerk or the like, to which my fortune etc. condemns me and would willingly risk my life though not my character to exalt my station. I'm confident, Ned that my youth excludes me from any hopes of immediate preferment nor do I desire it, but I mean to prepare the way for futurity. I'm no philosopher you see and may be justly said to build castles in the air.

Hamilton finished by asserting with excusable youthful exuberance, "I wish there was a war." The young man had read enough books and heard enough talk in the port city to know that warfare was perhaps the best means to achieve lasting glory and fame. Performing great courageous and valiant deeds on the battlefield was a sure path to win honor. Hamilton was correct enough, but, in his present circumstances, was far away from winning the objects of his ambitions.

While he was dreaming of a better life, Hamilton was fortunate to have the support of several wealthy patrons who wished to provide opportunities for the brilliant young man. Reverend Hugh Knox was a Presbyterian minister who served as a mentor to Hamilton and exposed him to a wider world of ideas. Knox discussed religion and the ideas of the Scottish Enlightenment with the eager young man who devoured books in the minister's impressive library. Knox also shared his experiences at the College of New Jersey (Princeton) and encouraged Hamilton to seek an education. The minister raised the funds with Cruger and other merchants to send their young protégé to North America. In late 1772, Hamilton thus boarded a ship bound for the American colonies with the promise of an education and a chance to seek a better destiny for an orphaned bastard. What he would make of those opportunities was entirely up to him.

CHAPTER 2

THE EDUCATION
OF A PATRIOT

O nce he landed in America, Hamilton traveled to New York
with letters of introduction, ready to begin his studies. He
arrived at a time of relative calm in imperial relations with
the British after nearly a decade of resistance to taxes and tyranny.
In New York, he had the help of several of Cruger's business partners
and befriended members of the New York Sons of Liberty including
Hercules Mulligan.

With so many deficiencies in his education, Hamilton was unprepared to take the Princeton entrance exams. He studied at Elizabethtown Academy in New Jersey to remedy those defects. The Livingston
clan welcomed Hamilton and acquainted him with the patriot circle at
its manor, Liberty Hall. Hamilton met several individuals who would
become consequential figures in the Revolutionary War and founding,
including William Alexander, Lord Sterling, Elias Boudinot, John Jay,
and Aaron Burr. This heady culture of civility and wealth attracted
Hamilton and reinforced his study with Reverend Knox about the
dissenting traditions of Whig politics and Presbyterian religion. With
his strong work ethic, Hamilton completed the course of study in six
months and was ready to enter Princeton.

Hamilton met with the distinguished president of Princeton,
Reverend John Witherspoon. Witherspoon was a giant of Scottish
Enlightenment philosophy, a devout Presbyterian, and a fierce patriot

who trained numerous American statesmen who became leaders in the revolutionary movement, including James Madison. Hamilton arrogantly dictated the terms of his education to President Witherspoon. Hamilton offered to complete the Princeton curriculum in a mere two years. There is little doubt that Hamilton was not merely boasting and could have completed the proposed program because of his work ethic and genius. Reverend Witherspoon politely but firmly declined the young man's request.

Hamilton decided to attend King's College (now Columbia) in New York instead. King's College may have been a loyalist institution differing in character from Princeton, but Hamilton nevertheless received a first-rate classical education. The president of the college was Dr. Reverend Myles Cooper, who was a staunch Anglican and Tory. As his essays would soon indicate, he became a close student of the writings of Enlightenment thinkers John Locke, David Hume, and Sir William Blackstone. Hamilton also joined one of the debating societies that were popular public arenas to exchange ideas in the eighteenth century.

The hustle and bustle of the commerce in the growing cosmopolitan port attracted him for its many opportunities for a young man on the make. New York City was a bustling city of twenty thousand inhabitants that was much larger than Christiansted in St. Croix. However, there was something familiar about the global commerce and the diversity of ethnicities and languages. Hamilton was drawn to New York City and would settle there.

While Hamilton was buried in his books, the patriot movement was emboldened by the opposition to the Tea Act and the Boston Tea Party in December 1773. In the spring of 1774, the British punished Boston with the Coercive Acts that stripped Massachusetts of self-government, trial by jury, and trade. New York was one of the epicenters of resistance against British tyranny and, in late May, the leaders of the Sons of Liberty, Alexander McDougall and Isaac Sears, organized a group of patriots into a Committee of Fifty-One that expressed its common cause with Boston. On July 4, the committee selected delegates to the upcoming Continental Congress, and two days later, organized a mass meeting to protest British actions.

The immigrant student and his Sons of Liberty friends were swept up in the patriot furor. Hamilton attended the public meeting and addressed the crowd. He called on his fellow New Yorkers to forge a common cause with their Boston brethren. He urged a colonial boycott of British goods to protest the violation of American liberties. The crowd was amazed to hear such an eloquent articulation of American principles and shouted, "It's a collegian!"

However, over the next several months, Hamilton penned some important patriotic pamphlets that showed his support of the cause and his remarkable genius even more than the speech he had delivered. Just as the crowd could not believe that a college student had delivered such oratory, many readers, including President Cooper, could not believe that Hamilton was the author of the pamphlets.

The Continental Congress met during the fall of 1774 to consider measures to combat the Coercive Acts. The delegates agreed to a ban on trade with Great Britain and a declaration of rights. They also decided to meet the following spring to assess the situation that was unfolding. Most hoped the British would see reason, rescind the hated measures, and work out a compromise.

A month after the Congress disbanded in October, Anglican priest and Tory New Yorker Samuel Seabury published a pamphlet attacking Congress titled *Free Thoughts on the Proceedings of the Continental Congress* under the pseudonym of A. W. Farmer. Painting himself as an ordinary farmer, Seabury denounced the continental boycott as an "abominable scheme." The wealthy delegates, he thought, could easily pay the "trifling tax" on tea. He labeled the members of Congress as lawless, predatory politicians hurting the interests of ordinary colonists. In short, they were a "venomous brood of scorpions."

The seventeen-year-old Hamilton defended Congress with a torrent of words that he published only weeks later as *A Full Vindication of the Measures of Congress*. The title alone divulged Hamilton's intention to defend the honor of the Continental Congress from Seabury's vicious assaults. The pamphlet opened by calling A. W. Farmer presumptuous for insulting the respectable delegates who assembled in Philadelphia. The dignified and honorable members of Congress pursued measures to secure the natural rights and liberties of the American colonists.

After another reply by Seabury, Hamilton published an even lengthier pamphlet in early 1775. *Farmer Refuted* was a masterpiece of natural rights political philosophy heavily influenced by Enlightenment thinking. He argued for the universal natural rights of all humans. "The sacred rights of mankind are not to be rummaged for, among old parchments, or musty records. They are written, as with a sun beam, in the whole volume of human nature, by the hand of divinity itself; and can never be erased or obscured by mortal power." Drawing on Blackstone, Locke, and other thinkers, he wrote that the purpose of government was to protect those rights. "The origin of all civil government, justly established, must be a voluntary compact between the rulers and ruled . . . for the security of the absolute rights of the latter." Any attempt to usurp those rights would be a violation of the social compact and compel the sovereign people to rebel against tyranny.

In April, the Revolutionary War broke out when blood was shed at Lexington and Concord. On the night of April 18, British General Thomas Gage sent infantry through the Massachusetts countryside to seize colonial weapon caches and capture the prominent rebels Samuel Adams and John Hancock. After the redcoats killed eight colonists at Lexington, they marched on Concord. Fighting erupted on the Concord Bridge, and the colonists chased the redcoats back to Boston with hundreds of casualties on both sides. The Revolutionary War had begun.

Thousands of colonial militiamen marched to Boston to confront Gage's armies, while others remained in their colonies to train and prepare for war. New Yorkers mobilized and raided the city arsenal to seize weapons for their defense. Hamilton and some of his classmates enthusiastically volunteered for a militia company called the Corsicans and spent a great amount of time drilling between classes. They had the revolutionary slogan "Liberty or Death" sewn onto their caps. Hamilton and the other young men were prepared to sacrifice their lives for their sacred liberties, and sought lasting glory on the battlefield.

New York, however, was divided over the war as one of the centers of Toryism in America. The Sons of Liberty carefully orchestrated mobs that swept through the streets and carried out acts of retribution against Loyalists. When these riots targeted Tories and their property, Hamilton stood for the rule of law. One night in May, an angry mob of hundreds assembled, bent on tarring and feathering President Cooper. Hamilton and his friend Robert Troup defended Cooper's life from the passions of the mob. Hamilton warned the throng that any violence would "disgrace and injure the glorious cause of liberty." While the speech did little to sway the mob, Cooper was able to use the diversion to escape into the night and find refuge on a British warship.

A few months later, Hamilton became involved in another incident to preserve the rule of law against the whims of the mob. Connecticut militiamen seized pamphleteer Samuel Seabury and printer James Rivington, who had published Seabury's writings. The mob marched into Rivington's print shop and smashed his press. Hamilton harangued this crowd, albeit unsuccessfully. Hamilton explained his position to John Jay. "I am always more or less alarmed at everything which is done of mere will and pleasure without any proper authority." He continued: "In times of such commotion as the present, while the passions of men are worked up to an uncommon pitch, there is great danger of fatal extremes. The same state of the passions which fits the multitude, who have not a sufficient stock of reason and knowledge to guide them . . . very naturally leads to a contempt and disregard for all authority."

In June, the British made three assaults against the colonists entrenched atop Breed's Hill. The British eventually captured the hill in the Battle of Bunker Hill but at the great cost of one thousand casualties. The British were shocked that the citizen-soldiers stood and fought the more disciplined, professional British army. As a result, the war in Boston was stalemated for the next nine months until the British generals decided to evacuate the city.

In August, the members of the New York Provincial Congress feared that the British would seize the cannon at the battery at Fort George and ordered them removed. Hamilton joined other daring classmates who went to the battery. They had almost completed their mission when they attracted the attention of the British navy, which was patrolling New York waters unchallenged. An armed barge discovered the Americans and bombarded the battery to stop them. The students traded some ineffective fire and worked feverishly to withdraw the last few guns. The warship, HMS *Asia*, then turned broadside and unleashed a thunderous barrage that set fire to a tavern and sent the students scurrying. Hercules Mulligan left Hamilton's musket behind during the chaos, and Hamilton rushed back to recover it under intense fire. It may have been a foolhardy move, but, in his first minor action of the war, Hamilton proved his mettle and did not flinch.

The siege of Boston produced a lull in New York during the late autumn in which Hamilton had time to pen a series of "Monitor" essays. Hamilton wrote that the British had pushed their tyrannical measures too far and that it was too late to retract them now that the war had started. The British had staked their national honor upon squelching the American rebellion and could not turn back. He urged his countrymen to meet the danger with manly and honorable virtue, and warned against excess caution and timidity. These vices would lead to a dishonorable submission to arbitrary rule that would lower the character of Americans from freemen to slaves. Echoing Patrick Henry's "Give Me Liberty or Death" speech, Hamilton wrote that Americans must decide whether to "lead an honorable life or to meet with resignation a glorious death." For young Hamilton, an honorable life lived for a glorious purpose was the only one worth living.

In February 1776, the Scottish and Presbyterian patriot Alexander McDougall recommended Hamilton to captain an artillery company recently raised by the New York Provincial Congress. Hamilton mustered the company and fought to put it on an equal footing with units in the Continental Army. Hamilton had no more experience than the merchants, booksellers, and artisans who comprised most of the American officer corps, but he was a natural leader and a quick study. He would have to prove himself in battle if he wanted opportunities for promotion.

In the wake of his appointment, Hamilton reflected on the path on which he was embarking in a public letter. He was willing to sacrifice for the sacred cause of liberty and die for his honor. "I am going into the army and perhaps ere long may be destined to seal with my blood the sentiments defended by my pen. Be it so, if heaven decree it. I was born to die and my reason and conscience tell me it is impossible to die in a better or more important cause."

CHAPTER 3

THE CROSSING

On the night of March 4, a couple thousand American troops marched up to Dorchester Heights overlooking the British positions in Boston and fortified the hill. When first light broke, the British were surprised to see the American position on the hill from which the colonists could fire the guns that Henry Knox valiantly rescued from Fort Ticonderoga. The British generals met and decided to withdraw from Boston and sail to Nova Scotia, where they awaited reinforcements and supplies as part of a massive invasion to crush the rebellion.

General George Washington predicted that the British would invade New York. The British would have great advantages there. The Royal Navy would have uncontested naval superiority around the waters of Manhattan and would be able to land troops virtually anywhere. Washington later considered burning it to deny it to the British, but Congress rejected the idea. The commander-in-chief had no choice but to defend an indefensible city and was anxious his army might be trapped and defeated. Even if he saved the army, the British would cut the colonies in two and isolate New England when they took the city. He had sent former British military officer Charles Lee to strengthen the city's fortifications. Once the British evacuated Boston, Washington moved his army to New York to await the coming onslaught.

Alexander Hamilton was training his artillery company when the Continental Army marched into the city. General Nathanael Greene may have noticed the young captain and invited him to dinner. Elias Boudinot, a well-placed member of the Livingston circle, also approached the talented young man and offered him a position as an aide-de-camp to Brigadier General Lord Sterling. Hamilton knew these men from his time at Elizabethtown Academy and understood that such an assignment was an honorable position and a great opportunity. After deliberating over the offer, he turned it down because he wanted to win glory fighting in the war rather than serve as a staff officer. He went back to training his men, knowing that war was coming to New York.

Defensive preparations continued until the British sailed a vast armada of more than one hundred warships and transports into New York with thirty-two thousand redcoats and Hessian mercenaries. From their vantage point at the Battery, Hamilton and his men saw what appeared to be a forest of masts in the distance. On July 3, the enemy landed on Staten Island and began disembarking troops. They probably watched in awe and had a sinking feeling witnessing the military might of the British Empire.

Meanwhile, in Philadelphia, Congress adopted Richard Henry Lee's motion that "these United Colonies are, and of right ought to be, free and independent States," and two days later, the Declaration of Independence. On July 9, American soldiers in New York assembled to hear officers read the stirring words of the Declaration of Independence. A mob of soldiers and civilians celebrated independence by tearing down a statue of George III, which was melted down into 42,088 bullets. Hamilton was as exultant as any of the native-born Americans that his adopted country was fighting for Lockean natural rights principles and consensual self-government. But Hamilton and the soldiers on the ground in New York knew that they had to fight and defeat the British and their mercenaries to make independence a reality.

Hamilton got his chance a few days later. On July 12, the Royal Navy tested the defenses around New York while demonstrating its firepower. Two warships sailed toward the Battery and opened up with a few thunderous broadsides. Hamilton's company loaded their guns and prepared to return fire. Tragically, the guns misfired and exploded, killing several men. They acquitted themselves poorly in their disastrous first encounter. Even General Washington complained of their incompetence. For the commander-in-chief, it was a catastrophic way to begin hostilities; for Hamilton, the calamity was not the way to win the confidence of his superiors.

In late August, the British and Hessian army crossed to Long Island and attacked the Americans. The Battle of Long Island was a major debacle. The British launched a diversionary frontal assault against the Americans on the heights near Flatbush while turning the American flank. The defeat turned into a rout, as the British captured American generals and inflicted heavy casualties. Most of the American army narrowly escaped to Brooklyn Heights and across into Manhattan in great confusion with the British in pursuit.

The British drove the Continental Army across Manhattan into headlong retreat. Washington lamented, "Are these the men with whom I am to defend America?" Incredulous at disaster unfolding around him, Washington ignored the flying bullets and had to be roused from his stupor before he was captured. Hamilton courageously covered the retreat against the advancing enemy and was among the last troops fleeing from the British. The men in the artillery company had to abandon two guns to make their escape. They reached the relative safety of the defenses at Harlem Heights where the Americans were hastily erecting an earthen redoubt. It would be hard to imagine that Washington did not notice the daring and determination of the young man under fire.

On September 16, the Americans drove back a fierce British assault at Harlem Heights. Hamilton's artillery was folded into the Continental Army and placed under the command of former bookseller General Henry Knox. Washington was pleased the lines held but could not defend the area for long. Hamilton again covered the army while it withdrew across the Bronx River and marched into White Plains. Hamilton and most of the army continued across the Hudson River and into New Jersey.

The British chased the Americans and caught up to them at the Raritan River at New Brunswick. On December 1, Hamilton and his men delivered a "smart cannonade" against the enemy and helped the army escape the clutches of the British yet again. Hamilton impressed General Washington with "brilliant courage and admirable skill" during the action. But Washington's army was rapidly shrinking as thousands of enlistments expired and hundreds of men abandoned the cause and returned home.

Washington marched his army to the Delaware and crossed to the Pennsylvania side, while General Howe went into winter quarters and left a Hessian garrison guarding Trenton. During the next few weeks, militia units arrived and doubled the size of Washington's small army. Nevertheless, Washington needed a bold stroke to save his crumbling and demoralized army, especially before more enlistments expired on January 1.

Hamilton was in bed laid low by an illness but mustered the strength to participate in the planned crossing of the Delaware. He would not allow sickness to interfere with even a fleeting chance to win honor after months of humiliating retreats. On Christmas Day, he directed his men loading artillery guns, ammunition, and horses onto the large barges for the crossing. A nor'easter blew up and pelted the men with rain, sleet, and snow. Knox, Hamilton, and the artillerymen landed safely and incredibly without incident. They dragged the guns with great difficulty over the sloshy terrain in the dark. The men were lashed by arctic winds and freezing temperatures as they marched. Several wore bloody rags on their feet instead of shoes. Still, they somehow pulled the guns eight miles through the night in the blinding snow.

The exhausted Americans fell upon the sleeping Hessian garrison in the morning. The Americans had achieved complete surprise. The Hessians roused themselves and tried desperately to organize a counterattack. Hamilton and his men set up their guns on the main street and cut down the Hessians who were trying to form up. The German artillerymen struggled to return fire after their officer fled and their horses were spooked by the deafening American fusillades. They finally set up their guns and engaged the Americans in a sharp artillery duel. However, Hamilton's men quickly neutralized the enemy guns. The Americans won the great victory at Trenton that Washington badly needed. Hamilton had acquitted himself well and shared in the glory of the victory.

Washington led his army back across the Delaware and was determined to launch another attack. A patriotic appeal and a ten-dollar bounty persuaded over one thousand soldiers to stay on for another month. They made a second crossing and set up their defenses in Trenton in time to meet a British attack by some eight thousand redcoats and mercenaries under Cornwallis. Hamilton's artillery repulsed two enemy attacks across the Assunpink Creek bridge under a devastating hail of crossfire that turned the creek red with blood. Night fell, and Washington slipped out to attack Princeton. Hamilton and his men muffled the wheels on the gun carriages and again wrestled with them in the overnight march through snow and ice.

In the morning, the Americans had a sharp encounter with the British force. During sharp fighting between the advance elements of both armies, Washington rode through heavy fire as he rallied his men at the front lines. The Americans broke the British lines and captured Princeton. Hamilton again played an important role in the battle and supposedly fired a shot that beheaded a portrait of George II in Nassau Hall at Princeton. Hamilton later wrote that the victories at Trenton and Princeton were the "dawnings of the bright day which afterwards broke forth with such resplendent luster."

Hamilton had performed admirably in several battles over the previous six months both in ignominious retreat and in glorious victory. Washington and his officers noted that he was a courageous young man and consistently cool under fire. One officer testified: "I noticed a youth, a mere stripling, small, slender, almost delicate in frame, marching beside a piece of artillery with a cocked hat pulled down over his eyes, apparently lost in thought, with his hand resting on the cannon and every now and then patting it as he mused, as if it were a favorite horse or a pet plaything."

The Continental Army went into winter quarters at Morristown, where Washington invited the valiant young artilleryman to join his staff as an aide-de-camp with a promotion to lieutenant colonel. Washington was overwhelmed by his responsibilities and sought talented individuals who could free him up to concentrate on strategy. He was an excellent judge of character and promoted numerous individuals to positions based upon talent and virtue rather than their aristocratic family connections and wealth.

In March 1777, Hamilton joined the staff with mixed feelings. He was honored by the offer to join Washington's staff. The position offered unlimited possibilities for upward mobility and to influence the highest levels of decision making in the Continental Army. On the other hand, Hamilton realized that accepting the position would impede his desire to win honor in combat. Nevertheless, he accepted the invitation and spent countless hours with the other aides working and socializing informally with each other and the general.

Hamilton became a trusted and indispensable aide almost immediately. His early experience as a clerk in the mercantile business served him well to bring administrative genius to the staff. He had an incisive mind and could soon read Washington's thoughts as he was entrusted with writing important correspondence with leading national and state political figures in Washington's name. As Hamilton wrote: "I find he is so much pestered with matters which cannot be avoided that I am obliged to refrain from troubling him on the occasion, especially as I conceive the only answer he would give may be given by myself." Fellow aide and friend Robert Troup noted how crucial Hamilton was to Washington and to the job. "The pen for our army was held by Hamilton; and for dignity of manner, pith of manner, and elegance of style, General Washington's letters are rivalled in military annals."

CHAPTER 4

WASHINGTON'S AIDE

A new campaigning season opened in the late spring of 1777. Hamilton was at General Washington's side as the commander formulated strategy and wrestled with Congress and the states for more supplies. British leadership for their part were at odds over strategy and pursued an incoherent strategy that mostly served the egos of the leading generals. William Howe was intent on marching on Philadelphia and seizing the largest American city and unofficial capital though the purpose was largely unclear. General John Burgoyne prepared an expedition southward from Canada into New York State through Lake Champlain to Albany, thereby isolating the seedbed of the revolt in New England. General Henry Clinton remained in New York City with a garrison of troops and no real intention of supporting the campaigns of either. With Generals Schuyler and Horatio Gates preparing to counter Burgoyne's move in upstate New York, the main Continental force tried to prevent the capture of Philadelphia.

Washington rushed thousands of Continentals northward to meet the threat, and Hamilton feared the loss of his adopted home state. "A state which I consider, in a great measure, as my political parent. . . . I agree with you that the loss of your state would be a more affecting blow to America than any that could be struck by Mr. Howe to the southward," he wrote. Nevertheless, he and others squarely placed the lion's share of blame for the recent loss of Fort Ticonderoga on his future father-in-law, Philip Schuyler, and commander of the Northern

Department. Hamilton wrote, "I have always been a very partial judge of General Schuyler's conduct and vindicated it frequently, but I am at last forced to suppose him inadequate." In early August, Congress replaced Schuyler with the wildly popular General Horatio Gates, who was an experienced and ambitious former officer in the British Army. Meanwhile, Washington contended with General Howe's army.

In July, General Howe belatedly put out to sea and sail around to confuse the Americans as to his ultimate target rather than simply marching on Philadelphia. After a month at sea, the weakened redcoats sailed up the Chesapeake and finally landed in Maryland. Washington understood the symbolic importance of Philadelphia and sought to defend the city. He was also an aggressive commander who wanted to build on his military successes from the previous winter by defeating the British on the field of battle. Hamilton marched with the Continental Army through the city to bolster the morale of citizens and members of Congress. He was joined by two newcomers to the army who were his fast friends.

Colonel John Laurens was the son of South Carolina congressman and wealthy planter, Henry Laurens. Laurens was educated in Geneva, where he learned French and developed an Enlightenment antipathy to slavery, and in London at the Inns of Court, Middle Temple, where he studied law. He was a young romantic who was stirred by Thomas Paine's fiery pamphlet, *Common Sense*, and by the appeal to the rights of mankind in the Declaration of Independence. He eagerly wanted to serve in the glorious cause of liberty being fought in his native land. When young Laurens arrived back in America, his father used his connections to secure the young man a position on Washington's staff as an aide. Henry Laurens had hoped that his son would be safe in a staff position, but he underestimated the romantic ardor of this young revolutionary for battle. Despite the tinge of nepotism, the young man would have to prove his ability to Washington, who wanted men of talent and virtue on his staff and commanding troops.

Hamilton and John Laurens struck up an intimate and abiding friendship as Washington's aides. The pair of young men were nearly the same age, both brilliant, and temperamentally the same. They were zealous eighteenth-century revolutionary romantics who yearned for the glories of honor and reputation in battle and even in death. They wore their heart on their sleeve and were frequently given to sharing exaggerated, florid expressions of love for each other and their cause. For example, Hamilton wrote to Laurens: "Till you bade us adieu, I hardly knew the value you had taught my heart to set upon you. Indeed, my friend, it was not well done. . . . You should not have taken advantage of my sensibility to steal into my affections without my consent." Historian Richard Brookhiser judiciously notes that these effusive expressions were probably a product of a sentimental age rather than evidence of a homosexual relationship, but we cannot be sure. They served together in Washington's service both at headquarters and occasionally on the battlefield. They both spoke French and served as translators and interpreters for Washington as the French were not-so-secretly aiding the American cause and Frenchmen were coming to America in increasing numbers seeking to take part in its revolution for liberty and the rights of man.

The Marquis de Lafayette had recently arrived in America aboard *Victoire*, a ship he bought to take him to the country "that animates me for their happiness, their glory, and their liberty." Lafayette was a fabulously wealthy noble and officer in the French Army. Lafayette and many of his countrymen were smitten by Enlightenment ideals of liberty and swept up in the American cause. Washington was frustrated with the number of foreign officers that Congress foisted upon him, but Lafayette received a commission in late July. Risking his life and limb, and serving in a disinterested manner without pay, Congress made Lafayette an honorary major general and praised "his great zeal to the cause of liberty." Washington changed his tune and warmly welcomed Lafayette in August once he ascertained the young man's quality.

Hamilton found another kindred spirit in Lafayette. Hamilton and Lafayette were both foreigners who sailed for America and were effusive believers in American ideals of liberty and self-government. They were born the same year and both deeply committed to the notions of personal honor and winning glory. The triumvirate of young men conversed in French and were indispensable links for Washington in his relationship to the French, especially after the French Alliance. Lafayette called himself "a friend who loves you tenderly" as he exchanged romantic gushes with Hamilton about their friendship and

American liberty. Lafayette had the coveted position of line officer commanding troops that Hamilton wanted. But Hamilton did not let it become a source of contention in their relationship. Instead, he admired the Frenchman and longed for the same glory.

Hamilton was surprised that Howe did not march toward Albany and link up with Burgoyne. Hamilton feared that if Howe were to "cooperate with Burgoyne, it would demand our utmost efforts to counteract them." Howe decided to advance on Philadelphia with the objectives of destroying Washington's army, taking the capital where Congress sat, and forcing the Americans to sue for a settled peace. But his goals were uncoordinated with the rest of the British army, and he inexplicably moved late in the campaigning season.

On September 11, the two armies clashed at Brandywine Creek. Washington held the high ground and thought his flanks were adequately covered because he incorrectly assumed that there were no other crossings above the main ford. Washington even dismissed repeated reports that the British were turning his flank. Howe knew better and set out with a massive force of 8,500 under Cornwallis early that morning. The redcoats were hidden from the Americans by a shroud of fog. Washington fell for a frontal feint and only belatedly realized his flank was in danger, so he rushed Nathanael Greene to cover it. The Americans barely arrived in time and held the line against a fierce British assault. By day's end, the out-generaled Washington had suffered grievous casualties in his army. Moreover, Hamilton's new friend, Lafayette, was wounded in the leg.

After suffering a strong blow and knowing that Philadelphia was endangered, Washington dispatched Hamilton on two important missions. First, Hamilton and "Light-Horse" Harry Lee raced with eight cavalrymen to burn the flour mills along the Schuylkill River to deny them to the advancing British. They were carrying out the task when some British troops began firing on them. While Lee and several of the men raced off on their horses, Hamilton and three men attempted to cross the river on a flatboat in a highly exposed position. With nowhere to hide, one of the soldiers was killed and one was wounded. Hamilton ordered them into the swollen river, and a strong current swept them away. A waterlogged Hamilton sent a message to John Hancock warning Congress to evacuate. Sleeping congressmen were roused from their beds in the middle of the night and grabbed a few belongings as they fled out of town.

Washington entrusted Hamilton with an even more critical mission that required great prudence. The general invested his aide with extraordinary powers to procure blankets, clothing, horses, and military stores for the undersupplied army. The commander warned Hamilton to execute the task with "as much delicacy and discretion as the nature of the business demands." If Hamilton was imperious with the civilians, Washington predicted it could "involve the ruin of the army, and perhaps the ruin of America." With the survival of the army and the national honor at stake, Hamilton and one hundred soldiers rushed to the city and commandeered the supplies from the republican citizenry. He made a careful accounting of the requisitioned materials and issued receipts for the goods. The supplies were immediately sent along the Delaware to the army. Only a few days later, Howe marched the British Army into Philadelphia.

In early October, Washington felt the time was ripe to launch another attack. He struck at part of Howe's army at Germantown with four columns advancing in an intricate maneuver beginning with an exhausting fifteen-mile nighttime march through unfamiliar terrain. The lines became confused as the American commanders lost contact with each other, especially when a thick morning fog settled over the land. While parts of the American attack went better than planned and pushed the British back, most of the assault was a disaster. Some units were lost and never made it to the battle; others arrived too late. The timetable went completely awry. Worst of all, one hundred redcoats took refuge in a stone house that was impervious to repeated American infantry and artillery assaults. Washington lost another 1,200 men, compounding the losses suffered at Brandywine. Members of Congress grew frustrated with Washington's performance, especially after a brilliant victory at Saratoga.

In New York, Burgoyne crossed the Hudson and slowly advanced on Albany without reinforcements from Howe or Clinton. The Americans won two spectacular victories at Freeman's Farm and then at Bemis Heights with the help of Daniel Morgan's Virginia sharpshooters and the intrepid leadership of Benedict Arnold. On October 17, Burgoyne surrendered, and the Americans bagged 5,900 prisoners and their arms. The Battle of Saratoga was a turning point in the war because diplomat Benjamin Franklin used the victory to negotiate a treaty of alliance with the French on February 6, 1778. France recognized American independence and sent an army, navy, and sorely needed arms and supplies. Americans celebrated Gates as a great hero.

Without skipping a beat, in November, Washington dispatched Hamilton to Gates to wrest away some of the Continental troops from the victorious northern army. Washington wanted to press the attack against Howe's army. The mission once again demonstrated Washington's great faith in Hamilton's abilities. The aide would have to summon every ounce of authority to contend with the haughty Gates, who would predictably be even more arrogant after Saratoga. Hamilton had orders to "deliver my sentiments upon the plan of operations" against Howe and express Washington's firm desire that the reinforcements "be immediately put in motion to join this army."

Hamilton mounted his horse and raced to Albany in only a few days. He stopped briefly at Fishkill on the Hudson and conferred with General Israel Putnam to send a few brigades and several hundred militia to Washington. Although Hamilton acted here on his own, he thought it was consistent with the wishes of the commander-in-chief. Hamilton felt honor-bound to submit his actions to his superior for censure, knowing that Washington would endorse the justice and necessity of his actions. "I concluded you would not disapprove of a measure calculated to strengthen you, thought but for a small time, and have ventured to adopt it on that presumption," he wrote.

Hamilton galloped into Albany and met resistance from Gates, who was basking in his glory. The general was not prepared to receive demands from a young aide even if the orders came from above. The two butted heads over the troops. Gates offered a sop of one brigade. Hamilton rejected the small concession and asked for two. Hamilton complained that it was "by far the weakest of the three now here." He believed that Gates was duty-bound to surrender the troops requisitioned by the commander-in-chief. Hamilton reported to Washington that, "I used every argument in my power to convince him of the propriety" of the demands, "but he was inflexibly in the opinion that two brigades at least of Continental troops should remain in and near the place." He considered Gates an impudent rascal for disregarding Washington's orders. For his part, Gates told Washington he felt insulted taking orders from some young aide. "I believe it is never practiced to delegate that dictatorial power to one aide-de-camp sent to an army 300 miles distant." Yet Washington had empowered Hamilton with exactly those powers, and expected that his orders were followed. In the end, Hamilton wrestled two brigades from Gates.

While in Albany, Hamilton dined at the Schuyler mansion and met the general's second daughter, twenty-year-old Eliza. She came from an excellent family and was remarkably beautiful. He would soon have an opportunity to meet her again, and when he did, he would fall deeply in love.

Hamilton discovered that Putnam had not sent the troops to Washington as promised. He delivered a stern lecture expressing his astonishment that Putnam had seemingly not taken any steps to comply with their agreement, which was a breach of honor. Putnam was also frustrating Washington's plans and consequently "the cause of America is put to the utmost conceivable hazard." Hamilton asked pardon for being so abrasive but explained that his passions were animated by a concern for "a matter where I conceive this continent essentially interested." In other words, the national honor was at stake.

General Washington assured his aide that he had acted with honor and propriety in carrying out his orders. "I approve entirely of all the steps you have taken and have only to wish that the exertions of those you have had to deal with had kept pace with your zeal and good intentions." That was all Hamilton needed to hear.

However, the frenetic pace that Hamilton had kept severely compromised his health. As he rode back to camp, he suffered fevers and a variety of other ailments that kept him bedridden for weeks at a time. He finally recovered and gathered enough strength to complete the final leg of his journey at Valley Forge on January 20, 1778.

While Hamilton was away on his errand, Washington heard rumors circulating in Congress that he might be replaced by Gates. In November, Washington received a copy of a letter that Brigadier General Thomas Conway had written to Gates stating that, "Heaven has been determined to save your country or a weak general and bad counselors would have ruined it." Conway was a French officer of Irish descent who was roundly dismissed as an arrogant narcissist by

Washington and his aides. Washington said Conway's "importance in the army, exists more in his imagination than in reality." Hamilton agreed, severely indicting Conway's character: "He is one of the vermin bred in the entrails of this chimera dire, and there does not exist a more villainous calumniator or incendiary." Washington directly confronted the pair and demanded satisfaction. He warned that such disloyalty caused dissention in the army and gave "a gleam of hope to the enemy."

On December 8, Gates wrote Washington a spluttering defense and tried to shift the blame to Hamilton during his recent visit. Gates explained that Hamilton had been left alone in his office for over an hour, rifled through his papers, and made a copy of the letter. "I conjure your excellency to give me all the assistance you can in tracing out the author of the infidelity which put extracts from General Conway's letters to me into your hands. Those letters have been *stealingly copied*." Gates implored Washington to help him discover the "wretch who may betray me," but Washington was having none of it. Washington forwarded the letters to Congress, and his allies in Congress and the army rallied to his defense. Sensitive about slights to his honor, Hamilton never forgave Gates. "I am his enemy personally for unjust and unprovoked attacks against my character."

Although historians doubt whether the "Conway Cabal" actually amounted to a real conspiracy against Washington, the general thwarted his rivals and emerged from the affair with a renewed public reputation. Hamilton certainly thought that there was a real conspiracy to unseat Washington. "I have discovered such convincing traits of the monster that I cannot doubt its reality in the most extensive sense," he wrote. Fortunately, the plot "unmasked its batteries too soon . . . all the true and sensible friends to their country, and of course to a certain great man, ought to be upon the watch."

Washington was fighting against political machinations while desperately holding his army together. He had marched his army into the wooded wilderness of Valley Forge one month before Hamilton arrived. He kept the soldiers busy building huts, constructing defenses, patrolling, standing guard, and foraging for supplies. Still, the men were dissatisfied with the dearth of supplies that left them starving and freezing. The army did not have any meat, little flour, and few blankets. The soldiers angrily chanted "No meat! No meat!" while they consumed a diet of fire-cakes (baked flour and water). Soon typhus, scurvy, and camp fever ravaged the weakened soldiers and sent hundreds to the infirmary. Hamilton found the army in this terrible condition when he returned to camp.

In February, the heavy snow fell, and the emaciated men were too weakened to survive the plunging temperatures or resist disease. More than twenty-five hundred men died that winter. One thousand soldiers and hundreds of officers had already deserted the army. Washington and his aides debated what to do about the situation for hours. Hamilton thought the dire situation would have fatal consequences resulting in the destruction of the army and the war for independence. "At this very day, there are complaints from the whole line of having been three or four days without provisions. Desertions have been immense and strong features of mutiny begin to show themselves. It is indeed to be wondered at that the soldiers have manifested so unparalleled a degree of patience as they have." If Congress and the states did not act soon to supply the army, he pondered, "I know not how we shall keep the army together."

While waiting for more fortunate circumstances, Hamilton had some leisure time to read several works of history, philosophy, and finance and record observations about them. He applied the lessons learned to the contemporary situation. The national Congress was weak and depended upon requisitions to the states that often went unfulfilled, especially when the war came close to home. The Congress was ruled by "folly, caprice, a want of foresight, comprehension, and dignity." Even ordinary citizens supplying the army had their patriotism wax and wane according to their own difficulties, fluctuating market prices for goods, the falling value of the currency, and the proximity of the fighting. Hamilton began to see the necessity of a stronger central government to preserve the cause of liberty. For him, it was "infinitely more important to have a wise general council" in the Congress. Politicians must serve that national body with a continental vision rather than the narrow, local concerns of state legislatures. Most importantly, the honor of the new nation and government was at stake. As he told New York governor George Clinton, "I can never adopt the reasonings of some *American* politicians . . . that no regard is to be paid to national character or the rules of good faith." He feared that such conduct would "bring government at home in contempt." He lamented that they were making a dishonorable and calamitous start as a newly independent nation.

Hamilton thought often about upholding the national character during that winter. When Washington charged Hamilton with managing a prisoner exchange with the British, Hamilton discovered that members of Congress wanted the negotiations to fail so that they could blame the outcome of the British. Hamilton was disturbed that the Congress were ruining America's national reputation. He thought it a dishonorable course because "to commit such frequent breaches of faith" would "ruin our national character."

At Valley Forge, Hamilton and his fellow officers vented that Congress was promoting "every petty rascal who comes armed with ostentatious pretensions of military merit and experience." One such person was Baron Friedrich Wilhelm von Steuben, who had questionable credentials supposedly conferred by service in the Prussian Army. Nevertheless, Washington assigned von Steuben the task of disciplining and drilling the Continental Army. In mid-March, he began training a model company of one hundred men who would then train their own companies. Von Steuben spoke French and befriended Hamilton and Laurens, who enjoyed their time discussing Enlightenment ideas with the cultivated European. Hamilton thought highly of von Steuben as "a gentleman for whom I have a particular esteem." Hamilton helped von Steuben rewrite the army's drill manual to standardize procedures. He and Laurens interpreted the baron's commands for the men as they drilled and marched. The soldiers made dramatic progress in the discipline and maneuvers of an eighteenth-century European army. Hamilton praised von Steuben's results with the army and asserted that it was unquestionably due "to his efforts we are indebted for the introduction of discipline in the army." The Continental Army was ready to meet the British enemy again and eager to receive French aid.

Washington got his chance when the British under General Clinton, who had replaced Howe, decided to abandon Philadelphia and march his army overland back to New York. The long, lumbering line of redcoats proved an attractive target to Washington, who assembled a council of war. General Charles Lee and others opposed a general engagement, while the younger officers demanded an attack. Nathanael Greene argued that the public would think that the leadership was cowardly and that "our courage failed us" if they left the column unmolested. Hamilton was disgusted at their unmanly shirking from battle in even more colorful language. He said they "would have done honor" to a "society of midwives."

On June 28, Washington shadowed the enemy and dispatched a sizable force under Lee, who had equivocated about accepting command of a strike against the British rearguard until Lafayette was offered the honor. Lee finally attacked, and Clinton responded by reinforcing Cornwallis at the rear. With scorching temperatures approaching one hundred degrees, the American units were pushed back and soon fell into disarray. A confused Lee could not contain the rout as his army retreated chaotically. Hamilton rode up to the front line and confronted Lee, who asked, "Do I appear to you to have lost my senses?" Hamilton was flabbergasted by such an unseemly question from a leader in battle and found the answer "not a little embarrassing." Hamilton tried to rouse Lee from his stupor and take control. "I will stay here with you, my dear general, and die with you! Let us all die rather than retreat!" he assured Lee.

Washington was shocked to hear news of Lee's apparent breakdown and raced to the front. The commander rode up to Lee and cursed him as a "damned poltroon." Washington demanded to know "the meaning of this disorder and confusion!" Lee could only stammer a response, and an irate Washington relieved him on the spot. The general restored order to the lines by riding among them under fire and reorganizing the lines. Hamilton praised Washington's character and leadership for averting disaster. "I never saw the general to so much advantage. His coolness and firmness were admirable. He instantly took maneuvers for checking the enemy's advance and giving time for the army, which was very near, to form and make a proper dispensation." The commander skillfully brought order out of confusion. For his part, Hamilton had a horse shot out from under him while he was riding around the battlefield and dispatching Washington's orders. He had to be carried from the field and won a reputation among his fellow officers for feverish courage disregarding his own death in battle. After the rearguard battle, the British resumed their march to Sandy Hook and sailed to New York.

Hamilton thought that the army had performed well despite General Lee and believed that the training in Valley Forge had resulted in a more disciplined, professional army. "Our troops, after the first impulse from mismanagement, behaved with more spirit and moved with greater order than the British troops. You know my way of thinking of our army, and that I am not apt to flatter it. I assure you I never was pleased with them before this day."

In the aftermath, Lee complained to Congress about his treatment and labeled Hamilton and the other young loyalists (including Laurens and Lafayette) as "dirty earwigs." Lee demanded a court-martial from Washington, who readily complied, and the trial began six days later. Hamilton thought that Lee's actions in the Battle of Monmouth Courthouse were dishonorable and indefensible. Whatever the outcome of the trial, "I shall continue to believe and say his conduct was monstrous and unpardonable." Hamilton did not hold back when Lee cross-examined him, essentially calling Lee a coward to his face. "There appeared in you no want of that degree of self-possession, which proceeds from a want of personal intrepidity," he declared. Instead of being a cool and unruffled leader under fire, Hamilton testified that Lee became unhinged. Lee's cowardice resulted "from a temper not so calm and steady as is necessary to support a man in such critical circumstances." Lee was duly convicted and dismissed from the army for a year in disgrace.

The affair did not end there, however. Men on both sides defended their honor and that of their superiors. One of Lee's aides, Major John Skey Eustace, approached Hamilton rudely, and then refused Hamilton appropriate courtesy in addressing him, promptly turning on his heel and leaving the room. Laurens prodded his friend to respond to the personal insults and those against Washington, but Hamilton curiously declined. Laurens, however, challenged Lee to a duel. Later in the year, two days short of Christmas, Hamilton accompanied Laurens to the dueling ground and served as his second. Laurens wounded Lee in the side during the first exchange of fire, and Hamilton tried to dissuade a furious Lee from another round. Hamilton thought that the duel was conducted with "politeness, generosity, coolness, and firmness that ought to characterize a transaction of this nature." The duelists had behaved like men, and the code of honor was satisfied.

Only a few days after the British Army arrived back in New York, French Admiral Count d'Estaing sailed a French fleet into the waters of Sandy Hook. Hamilton served as one of Washington's interpreters with the French ally and won plaudits for his martial dignity and bearing. Washington sought to use the fleet in a combined operation against New York, but had to settle for an assault against a smaller British force in Newport, Rhode Island. When a hurricane broke up a naval encounter, d'Estaing sailed off to Boston. General John Sullivan angrily called off his attack and protested to Congress about the French admiral's cowardice. Washington had to smooth over relations as tempers cooled on both sides. Hamilton was sympathetic to the French and knew the significance of the alliance. "Their friendship is the pillar of our security," he observed. The war would shift to the south with a new British strategy, but Washington would also spend the next two years camped around New York, fruitlessly looking to find a way to utilize French military aid to crack that nut and end the war.

CHAPTER 5

REFLECTIONS AND FRUSTRATIONS

With the 1778 campaigning season for the year effectively over, Hamilton had more time to reflect on the American war effort. The first object of his attention was the American economy. Its currency was in shambles with rampant inflation. Hamilton attacked war profiteering in Congress in his Publius letters that fall. He accused Maryland congressman Samuel Chase of manipulating the flour market when Congress was going to purchase flour for the French fleet. Hamilton thought Chase's alleged actions were examples of extortion and avarice that were unbecoming to any citizen but particularly a delegate to Congress. As a statesman and leader of the new nation, Chase had sacrificed the public good and his public reputation for his "dishonest artifices." He had faith in the American people that "they will permit you any longer to abuse their confidence, or trample upon their honor."

During that fall, Laurens persuaded Hamilton to support a plan to strengthen the war effort and tie it to American principles of natural rights and liberty for all. Both young men were idealists dedicated to Enlightenment ideas about universal equality and the rights of man. They believed that slavery was a gross violation of those rights and debased human nature. African Americans were serving in the Continental Army and had proven their worth in the First Rhode Island

Regiment during the fighting in Newport. Laurens believed slavery contradicted the principles of the Declaration of Independence. He offered to use his inheritance to free slaves and arm them to fight for their own and American liberty. "I think that we Americans, at least in the Southern colonies, cannot contend with a good grace for liberty until we shall have enfranchised our slaves," argued Laurens.

Laurens was especially forceful in pushing the plan because the British captured Savannah at the end of the year. Laurens impulsively resigned as Washington's aide and rushed to South Carolina. The British had invaded and offered freedom to runaway slaves. Hundreds escaped to British lines and offered their services. Laurens feared that the British would threaten Charleston and developed a plan to raise four black battalions to fight in exchange for their freedom.

Hamilton concurred with the plan and wrote his fellow New Yorker, John Jay, the new president of Congress, and advanced the scheme for emancipation. "I have not the least doubt that the negroes will make very excellent soldiers with the proper management and I will venture to pronounce that they cannot be put in better hands than those of Mr. Laurens," he wrote. Hamilton believed that blacks were naturally equal to whites but had only been rendered subordinate by the condition of slavery. Slavery had degraded black manhood, but they could quickly recover their honor if given their freedom and an opportunity to prove themselves. "I think their want of cultivation (for their natural faculties are probably as good as ours) joined to that habit of subordination which they acquire from a life of servitude will make them sooner become soldiers than our white inhabitants." The emancipation plan was good for slaves and for the moral cause of the war for independence. It would "give them their freedom with muskets. This will secure their fidelity, animate their courage, and I believe will have a good influence upon those who remain by opening a door to their emancipation. . . . The dictates of humanity and true policy, equally interest me in favor of this unfortunate class of men." In short, it was the right thing to do.

The commander-in-chief was lukewarm on the idea but allowed the passionate young aides to propose the scheme to Congress. Congress endorsed the plan unanimously and recommended that South Carolina and Georgia "take measures immediately for raising three thousand able-bodied negroes" with compensated emancipation. The assemblies, however, reacted with predictable horror to freeing and arming their slaves, and killed the idea. Hamilton lamented to his friend that the chances of the plan coming to fruition were "very feeble." He reflected on human nature and thought that self-interest was trumping what was just. "Prejudice and private interest will be antagonists too powerful for public spirit and public good."

These philosophical musings about the failures of human nature depressed Hamilton. He believed that a lack of public spirit was dooming the American war effort, and that Americans were proving themselves unworthy of governing themselves. "Every [hope] of this kind my friend is an idle dream," he wrote Laurens. "There is no virtue [in] America. That commerce which presided [over] the birth and education of these states has [fitted] their inhabitants for the chain and . . . the only condition they sincerely desire is that it may be a golden one."

The Continental Army was shaping a vanguard of officers with a continental outlook. The failures of the republican government to exercise powers requisite to achieving its aims and winning respectability in the court of world opinion became a central focus for Hamilton and his fellow officers.

In early July 1779, Hamilton received an accusatory letter from Lt. Col. John Brooks that made him hot under the collar. A member of Congress, Francis Dana, had reportedly witnessed Hamilton say in a public coffeehouse that "it was high time for the people to rise, join General Washington, and turn Congress out of doors." Brooks further reported that Dana questioned Hamilton's patriotism and honor. "Mr. Hamilton could be no ways interested in the defense of this country; and, therefore, was most likely to pursue a line of conduct as his great ambition dictated."

Hamilton quickly fired back a livid response to Francis Dana regarding the "absolutely false and groundless" accusations. Hamilton defended his reputation and demanded an immediate retraction and apology. He followed with an undisguised warning that if he did not receive unqualified satisfaction from Dana, they would fight a duel. The participants avoided a duel, but Hamilton expended a great deal of energy defending his personal honor. Even during the war, he would tolerate no affronts to his honor and manhood.

That fall, Hamilton was falling into a deep despair about the American cause of liberty. The republican government was proving itself unequal to the task of winning the war. The virtue and patriotism of the American people and their leaders was disintegrating in his opinion. In September, he wrote Laurens: "Every [hope] of this kind my friend is an idle dream. There is no virtue in America. That commerce which presided the birth and education of these states has their inhabitants for the chain and . . . the only condition they sincerely desire is that it may be a golden one."

Hamilton went into winter quarters with the army at Morristown, where the Americans experienced a harsh winter with cold and snow that far surpassed that of the deadly winter at Valley Forge. Perhaps a combination of the miserable weather and the state of national affairs dampened his mood further around the turn of the year. "In short Laurens I am disgusted with everything in this world but yourself and very few more honest fellows and I have no other wish than as soon as possible to make a brilliant exit."

Hamilton's outlook was considerably cheered when Elizabeth Schuyler visited family in Morristown in February 1780. Several months before, he had written to Laurens about the characteristics he sought in a wife. He thought, "She must be young, handsome (I lay most stress upon a good shape), sensible (a little learning will do), well-bred (but she must have an aversion to the word *ton*), chaste and tender (I am an enthusiast in my notions of fidelity and fondness), of some good nature, a great deal of generosity." He hoped to shape her political opinions, and wanted a wife who believed in God moderately rather than fanatically. And, because money was important in this world, he hoped to marry into a wealthy family. "But as to fortune, the larger stock of that the better." His thoughts were pretty conventional for an ambitious young man in the eighteenth century. When Elizabeth socialized with Hamilton in camp, he found a woman who met and exceeded all his expectations. He seized his opportunity to court her.

Hamilton was immediately smitten by the beautiful, intelligent, and wealthy Eliza. One of his fellow aides remarked, "Hamilton is a gone man." He described her with gushing superlatives from his romantic and sentimental pen. "She is so strange a creature that she possesses all the beauties, virtues, and graces of her sex without any of those amiable defects . . . are esteemed by connoisseurs necessary shades in the character of a fine woman." He found her profoundly distracting to his military duties and joked that she should remove herself from his company.

Despite his humble origins, Hamilton was, in turn, quite a catch for Eliza and welcomed by her father into his family. He was brilliant, ambitious, and handsome. He had the confidence of General Washington and served on his staff. In short, he would make an excellent husband. The lovers were quickly engaged within a month. He told his dear friend Laurens that, "I give up my liberty to Miss Schuyler."

News from Laurens's home state was less happy for the American war effort. During the late winter, General Clinton sailed a force down to Charleston and landed to the south of the port. He and Cornwallis marched slowly toward the city and crossed the Ashley River in mid-March, while a British fleet entered Charleston harbor. American General Benjamin Lincoln did not want to risk his army but was pressured to hold the city by its leaders. The British laid a siege and bombarded the city. In mid-May 1780, Lincoln surrendered 6,700 soldiers and sailors, thousands of muskets, and hundreds of artillery pieces in a devastating loss.

Another reversal in the southern campaigns occurred in August at the Battle of Camden. General Horatio Gates won command of the Southern Department from Congress though he led a small army comprised mostly of militia. Impatient to win a victory reminiscent of the glory of Saratoga, Gates pursued the stronger British army and found it at Camden. Gates imprudently sent his unreliable militia against the British regulars, while his few Continentals opposed a weaker force of Tories fighting for the British. Gates ordered the militia forward, but the line crumpled even before the first shots were fired. He fruitlessly attempted to regroup his retreating army and then joined the stampede. Gates bolted and rode to Charlotte. Hamilton heard the news and roasted Gates for his cowardice and lack of honor in face of the enemy. "Was there ever an instance of a general running away, as Gates has done, from his whole army? One hundred and eighty miles in three days and a half. It does admirable credit to the activity of a man at his time of life." The American war effort was reaching its nadir.

Away from the main battlefields of the war, Hamilton spent a great deal of time that summer developing his ideas about the national government. "The fundamental defect is a want of power in Congress," he wrote. The Confederation was weak and at the mercy of the states. In his view, liberty was threatened more by a weak government that would dissolve into anarchy than a powerful central government. He supported the idea of a convention of the states to create a new plan of government with strengthened powers to govern the nation. He also wanted a strong executive to govern with greater vigor. To Laurens, Hamilton was more forthright about his fears: "I tell you necessity must force [the powers] down; and that if they are not speedily taken the patient will die." He was depressed, perhaps realizing his vision had little chance of coming to fruition. "I hate Congress—I hate the army—I hate the world—I hate myself. The whole is a mass of fools and knaves."

CHAPTER 6

BETRAYAL AND HEROISM

If military defeats and a pusillanimous national government were not dishonorable enough, the most sordid act of the American Revolution almost ruined the glorious cause in a single stroke. On September 25, Washington was traveling to the fort at West Point after a conference with Rochambeau about strategy. Hamilton and Lafayette accompanied the general. They went to West Point to inspect the fort because of its strategic importance on the Hudson. Washington had recently ordered the war hero General Benedict Arnold to take command of the fort. Hamilton rode ahead to Arnold's headquarters a few miles downriver with fellow aides James McHenry and Richard Varick to prepare a reception for the commander-in-chief at Arnold's home.

Arnold felt dishonored by his country after serving valiantly and patriotically during several key battles early in the war. Congress had passed him over for promotion, and his heroism at Saratoga was barely acknowledged. Moreover, he suffered a ghastly wound at Saratoga that left him hobbling on a cane. Washington assigned him as military governor of Philadelphia, where he courted a Tory Peggy Shippen, whom he married. Congress was now delinquent on his back pay and turned him down for a naval command in the Caribbean. Arnold felt abused and disrespected by his country for which he had shed his blood in its service. He decided to betray his country to the British for the promise of a princely sum of £20,000 and a command. Part of his planned treachery included kidnapping Washington, Hamilton, and the rest of the staff.

During breakfast with Washington's aides, Arnold received word that a spy named John Anderson had been captured behind American lines. The spy was actually British Major John André. Three militiamen had detained him near Tarrytown. He admitted he was a British officer and was taken into custody on the spot. The American soldiers searched him and discovered papers in his boot, which included the plans of West Point. They forwarded the papers to General Arnold, ignorant of the fact that he was a traitor.

Arnold thus learned of André's capture and became highly agitated. He excused himself and went upstairs to confer with Peggy. He furtively disappeared from the house and made his way to the British warship *Vulture*. Suddenly, Peggy began shrieking hysterically upstairs, and the men cautiously went upstairs. Peggy accosted them with accusations of wanting to kill her baby. She complained about hot irons burning her head and appeared deranged. Hamilton and the others unsuccessfully tried to calm her down. "It was the most affecting scene I ever was witness to," as Hamilton described it: "One moment she raved, another she melted into tears. Sometimes she pressed her infant to her bosom, and lamented its fate, occasioned by the imprudence of its father, in a manner that would have pierced insensibility itself."

When Washington and Lafayette finally arrived at the house angry that Arnold had not appeared for the inspection, Hamilton went downstairs and handed Washington the packets exposing the treason. Washington read them and exclaimed, "Arnold has betrayed us. . . . Whom can we trust now?" He recovered his senses enough to direct Hamilton and McHenry to give chase to Arnold. They jumped on their horses and rode several miles but could not catch the traitor. Hamilton had the wherewithal to order the Sixth Connecticut Regiment posted nearby to rush to defend the fortress should there be an imminent British attack. He dashed off a warning to Nathanael Greene that, "There has been unfolded at this place a scene of the blackest treason. I advise you putting the army under marching orders and detaching a brigade immediately this way."

Meanwhile, the general went upstairs to check on the condition of Arnold's wife, who was still hysterical and sobbing uncontrollably.

When Washington approached her, Peggy ranted, "No, that is not General Washington. That is the man who was a-going to assist Colonel Varick in killing my child." He tried unsuccessfully to console her.

Hamilton returned to the home to update Washington and received a note from Arnold trying to excuse his wife: "She is as good and as innocent as an angel and is incapable of doing wrong." The truth was that she was duping all of them by acting the part of a distressed wife to give Arnold the time to slip away to the British. The code of honor and chivalry blinded them to her deception. Hamilton thought Arnold was a dishonorable fiend for betraying his country and wife. Hamilton asserted he "wished myself her brother, to have a right to become her defender. . . . Could I forgive Arnold for sacrificing his honor, reputation, and duty, I could not forgive him for acting a part that must have forfeited the esteem of so fine a woman." Washington granted her a pass to return to Philadelphia even though she had conspired in Arnold's treason and escape.

Honor also dictated how Hamilton reacted to the fate of Major André. The Americans detained the British spy in a tavern in Tappan, New York. He was considered a spy because he wore civilian clothes, donned a disguise, and assumed an alias. Therefore, the court-martial found him guilty and sentenced him to death as a spy. Hamilton visited the prisoner several times and became enamored of André, who was an honorable British gentleman and exhibited the same romantic character that drew Hamilton to Laurens and Lafayette. Hamilton described André as "well improved by education and travel, [who] united a peculiar elegance of mind and manners and the advantage of a pleasing person." Hamilton pleaded André's case to Washington, arguing that André was not technically a spy and should be afforded the honor of a firing squad as a gentleman rather than face the gallows. Whatever Washington might have thought about André's honor, the commander-in-chief endorsed the spy's execution by hanging.

If anything, André's stoic and honorable acceptance of death only heightened Hamilton's deep regret. Hamilton noted that when André was led to the gibbet, he gracefully "bowed familiarly as he went along to all those with whom he had been acquainted in his confinement." The prisoner avowed, "I am reconciled to my death, though I detest the mode." Hamilton thought André went to his death with a "smile of complacency" and "serene fortitude of mind." He mounted the scaffold with great dignity, and even dramatically tightened the rope around his own neck and blindfolded himself. When asked to state any final words, André said, "Nothing but to request you will witness to the world that I die like a brave man."

After the fact, Hamilton was as smitten as ever with André as he mourned his death. "I am aware that a man of real merit is never seen in so favorable a light as seen through the medium of adversity," he bemoaned to Laurens. "The clouds that surround him are shades that set off his good qualities." Moreover, Hamilton was still resentful of Washington's decision two years later. He complained to Henry Knox that "it must still be viewed at a distance as an act of *rigid justice*." This remarkable respect for a spy who was involved in a treasonous plot that almost ruined the American cause was heavily colored by the lens of honor.

Hamilton had a joyous reprieve from the difficulties of military life and frustrations with the government when he journeyed to Albany for his wedding in late November. At noon on December 14, he married Elizabeth in the parlor of the Schuyler mansion. They honeymooned through Christmas, and the newlywed husband boasted that he was a "fanatic in love." In early January 1781, he reluctantly returned to military service, though his wife soon joined him in camp at New Windsor.

Hamilton found a new partner for life in Elizabeth, but he lost his main patron when he had a dramatic falling out with General Washington that sundered their close wartime relationship. Hamilton was always quick to defend his personal honor to a fault. Hamilton related the incident to Philip Schuyler, seeking to protect his honor and reputation with his father-in-law. He promised to give an honest accounting of the fissure to keep Schuyler's approval so soon after he married his daughter. "I wish what I have said to make no other impression than to satisfy you I have not been in the wrong," he wrote.

During one afternoon at headquarters in February 1781, Washington invited Hamilton to a private conference. Hamilton excused himself to deliver a letter and promised to return presently. The Marquis de Lafayette detained Hamilton for several minutes and left Washington fuming on the stairs. When Hamilton returned, Washington upbraided his young aide in an angry tirade. "Col. Hamilton . . . you have kept me waiting at the head of the stairs these ten minutes. I must tell you sir you treat me with disrespect." Hamilton was incredulous at such a blatant reprimand even from the commander-in-chief. "I am not conscious of it Sir, but since you have thought it necessary to tell me so we part." Washington angrily retorted, "Sir . . . if it be your choice," while Hamilton turned on his heel and stormed off.

Washington regretted that his volcanic temper had erupted with his aide and sent an underling to offer Hamilton an unprecedented opportunity to clear the air. Hamilton incredibly refused the meeting and stood fast in his desire to part company. He stayed on staff for a few weeks to maintain public appearances of unity but did leave. In this case, Hamilton put his personal reputation and honor above the American cause.

Hamilton thought that his role as an aide-de-camp was belittling and "unworthy of a courageous leader." He had joined Washington's staff because he had been enamored of Washington's presence and character. But he claimed that he had no amicable feelings toward the general. Hamilton unapologetically defended his honor whatever the consequences personally or for the war effort. "It was the deliberate result of maxims I had long formed for the government of my own conduct."

Hamilton was no longer a staff officer and had the opportunity to pursue a battlefield command that offered the chance to perform glorious deeds to win fame. He regretted wasting so much time as an aide and wanted to fight in the war. As he had written to Washington, "Sometime last fall when I spoke to your Excellency about going to the southward, I explained to you candidly my feeling with respect to military reputation and how much it was my object to act a conspicuous part in some enterprise that might perhaps raise my character as a soldier above mediocrity."

Schuyler reassured Hamilton that there was no impropriety in his actions. However, he gently counseled the young man that he was perhaps acting impetuously and should accept Washington's magnanimous apology for the public good. "Your quitting your station must therefore be productive of very material injuries to the public." Hamilton was critical to Washington's staff and even the French Alliance that he helped cultivate. He should consider the frailties of human nature and be more generous. Hamilton considered the advice and decided he could not forgive the slight. The result, as biographer Ron Chernow has written, was that, "One of the most brilliant, productive partnerships of the Revolution had ended."[1]

Hamilton spent the next several months at the Schuyler mansion and lobbying at the headquarters in upstate New York for a military command. He pressed his friends for any command he might win. Only two months after their falling out, Hamilton had the audacity to petition Washington for a combat position. He reminded the general impoliticly that he would have advanced in rank had he not served as a staff officer. Washington's blood was up at the young man's impertinence and shot back: "Your letter of this date has not a little embarrassed me." It was Washington's turn to feel his honor insulted. Hamilton did not relent in his attempts, and his insolence grew even worse in the coming months when he sent Washington a letter containing his commission with the obvious threat to resign if he did not receive a command. Finally, under the barrage of requests made by his persistent former aide, Washington relented and gave Hamilton a light-infantry command.

Whatever his role in the war, Hamilton tied his honor and fortunes to that of America and the national honor. In July, he started writing a series of six essays titled *The Continentalist*. Hamilton had served with the cadre of officers in the Continental Army who were molded by Washington's continental vision for the new nation and its military establishment. The wartime experience had shaped Washington's thinking about the need for a strong union of Americans united by a common vision and purpose. A strong national government with the requisite powers to govern the sovereign nation adequately was central to this vision. The Articles of Confederation had finally been ratified as a framework of government a few months before, but Hamilton was not impressed. "It will be an evil, for it is unequal to the exigencies of the war or to the preservation of the union hereafter."

In the *Continentalist* essays, Hamilton articulated a defense of this national outlook. He warned that Congress was too weak and ineffectual to govern because the states had jealously guarded their powers to the detriment of the whole during the war. The greatest defect was an inability of the central government to tax for revenue. Hamilton advocated a stronger central government with the power to tax, regulate trade, and establish a national bank to set the nation's finances on a proper foundation. The result would be a strong, reputable, and honorable nation at home and abroad. He wrote:

> There is something noble and magnificent in the perspective of a great federal republic, closely linked in the pursuit of a common interest, tranquil and prosperous at home, respectable abroad; but there is something proportionately diminutive and contemptible in the prospect of a number of petty states with the appearance only of union, jarring, jealous and perverse, without any determined direction, fluctuating and unhappy at home, weak and insignificant by their dissentions, in the eyes of other nations.

That summer and fall, the war sped toward a decisive confrontation that would determine the outcome. General Cornwallis, aided by traitor Benedict Arnold, had invaded Virginia, driven Lafayette from Richmond, and marched on Yorktown to establish a naval base for the British. In mid-August, French Admiral Francois-Joseph-Paul Count de Grasse sent word that he was sailing from the Caribbean to the Chesapeake with twenty-eight warships and three thousand soldiers. While Washington strongly desired a joint operation against New York, he reluctantly acceded to French General Count Rochambeau's argument to march against Cornwallis at Yorktown.

De Grasse's fleet sailed into the Chesapeake and soon engaged a smaller British fleet under Admiral Thomas Graves sent from New York to relieve Cornwallis. De Grasse drove the British off and then helped ferry troops marching down from around New York. Hamilton joined with the marching army and sailed around Annapolis, disembarking near Williamsburg on September 20. He had written to his wife before he departed, assuring her of his safety. "Cheer yourself with this idea, and with the assurance of never more being separated. Every day confirms me in the intention of renouncing public life, and devoting myself wholly to you. Let others waste their time and their tranquility in a vain pursuit of power and glory: be it my object to be happy in a quiet retreat with my better angel." Though his professions of love and devotion were sincere, he would not miss his shot at glory in what might prove to be the penultimate battle of the War for Independence. On September 28, he formed up with sixteen thousand Continental and French troops and advanced toward Yorktown.

The Allied armies arrived and sieged Yorktown, forcing Cornwallis to abandon his outer defenses. The French engineers directed the American sappers to dig a zigzag trench parallel with the British lines. The two armies exchanged artillery fire for several days early in October. As the moment neared when the Allied armies would launch their assault, Hamilton conferred with Lafayette and asked for the honor of leading the attack. Lafayette wanted to help his friend but deferred to Washington's judgment on the matter. Hamilton met with Washington and requested the command. Though we do not know the exact words that the pair exchanged, Hamilton did come out of the command tent excitedly announcing, "We have it! We have it!"

On October 14, Hamilton raced through the darkness as shells fell around them with three battalions, including the one led by Laurens. They fixed bayonets to surprise the enemy hidden behind the redoubts. He led from the front as he leaped onto a man's shoulders and onto the parapet. The American soldiers captured the redoubt quickly and took several prisoners. Meanwhile, the French assaulted an adjacent redoubt and took it after sharp fighting. As a result, the allies completed another parallel trench and brought up more guns. After a failed escape attempt, Cornwallis realized his position was hopeless and surrendered a few days later. On October 19, the British marched out and laid down their arms. The allies had won a decisive victory, and Alexander Hamilton was a great hero crowned in glory.

CHAPTER 7

THE NEWBURGH
CONSPIRACY

The American victory at Yorktown led to the long peace negotiations that would culminate in the 1783 Treaty of Paris with Great Britain. As the war drew down, Alexander Hamilton was only in his midtwenties and had a bright future ahead of him. He was still a young man in a hurry who wanted to make his mark on the world. His chosen profession took him to the familiar surroundings of a bustling international port. Hamilton's dedication to building a strong American republic constantly drew him into public affairs.

Hamilton became a war hero at the Battle of Yorktown and had served brilliantly for years at Washington's side. He had earned a furlough from the army after dedicating his life to his wartime service since 1776. In January 1782, the newlywed couple welcomed their first child, Philip, named in honor of Hamilton's father-in-law. The proud father bragged that his son had great prospects for "future greatness," and the growing family settled in comfortably at the Schuyler mansion. He reported that, "I lose all taste for the pursuits of ambition. I sigh for nothing but the company of my wife and my baby." This romantic musing was a genuine expression of domestic contentment, but he could not stay away from public life for long. Hamilton had time to reflect on his future career to support his family. He retired from the army a few months later and even declined a military pension in emulation of General Washington's virtuous disinterestedness. He decided to pursue a legal career.

The law had many attractions for Hamilton's brilliance and ambition. He may have joked to Lafayette that the law was the "art of fleecing my neighbors," but the pecuniary rewards of practicing law were an important consideration. Hamilton was also attracted to the competitive nature of the law as competing minds plumbed the depths of law and precedent to make arguments against opponents. A successful lawyer could win fame for arguing great cases dealing with important questions of justice to the public. Lawyers often served in state and local politics as well, and Hamilton knew he could not resist the temptations of public service and the possibility of lasting fame as a lawgiver in the ancient tradition. Moreover, as historian Forrest McDonald has argued, Hamilton acquired a "reverential enthusiasm for the law itself."[1] Society was built on law rooted in the principles of law, justice, order, stability, and virtue. These principles animated Hamilton's political philosophy, his vision for the United States, and his noble personal ambitions.

As was common in the eighteenth century, Hamilton prepared for the bar examination by reading the law rather than attending a law school. The New York Supreme Court paved the way for Hamilton to become a lawyer when it suspended the usual three-year apprenticeship in the law for soldiers whose study had been interrupted by the war. Hamilton may not have exactly qualified for the exemption, but he received the waiver anyway and promptly began his legal studies. Hamilton poured his unbridled energy into the endeavor as he had done at college and as he would do writing economic state papers in the Washington administration.

Beginning in April 1782, Hamilton consumed books voraciously from the law library of his friend, James Duane. Another friend, Robert Troup, recently passed the bar and tutored Hamilton. He read widely and deeply in the important legal theorists including Emmerich de Vattel and Samuel von Pufendorf on natural law and the law of nations, and English jurists Sir William Blackstone and Sir Edward

Coke. These standard sources further developed his thinking and reasoning in the natural law and natural rights philosophy of law. He also learned about ideas of judicial review in which judges could declare a statute void if it conflicted with higher natural law principles of justice.

Besides the high-minded ideas about law and justice, Hamilton studied the more practical and mundane topics of case precedents and legal procedure. He wrote a legal manual called "Practical Proceedings in the Supreme Court of the State of New York" as part of his preparation for the bar. It was nearly two hundred pages long and was read by other students as well. By July, the State of New York admitted the aspiring young lawyer to the bar. He launched a successful legal practice in New York City because of his strong political connections, a reputation for integrity, and his diligence in preparing for cases. Hamilton usually argued from first principles and used unassailable logic while attacking the flaws in his opponent's. His legal practice was highly lucrative but would always contend with the demands of his public service over the next two decades.

Hamilton's achievement in passing the bar so quickly was especially impressive considering his other projects and offices. In April and July, he had made final installments to his *Continentalist* essay series since the disgraceful state of the national government under the Articles of Confederation was never far from his mind. In May, Revolutionary Financier Robert Morris invited Hamilton to become the New York receiver of continental taxes. Hamilton had to turn Morris down, writing, "Time is so precious to me that I could not put myself in the way of any interruptions unless for an object of consequence to the public or to myself." A month later, Morris offered Hamilton more money, and despite his workload, he accepted. Hamilton was pessimistic about the prospect of success, however. "The whole system (if it may be called so) of taxation in this state is radically vicious, burthensome to the people and unproductive to government . . . there seems to be little for a Continental receiver to do."

Hamilton's fears of weakness in the central government were confirmed and amplified by experience trying to collect taxes in the state. He served for a total of four months and witnessed firsthand the inertia of the states in meeting their tax requisitions to the national government. He went to the state legislature and even persuaded the body to pass resolutions supporting increased national taxing power. The assembly even supported a motion for a convention to amend the Articles. As Hamilton told Morris, "The radical source of most of our embarrassments, is the want of sufficient power in Congress."

However, the state still did not meet its tax obligations to the national government, and the resolve for a convention was ignored. He complained to Morris, who shared his nationalist vision, that the New York government suffered "the general disease which infects all our constitutions—an excess of popularity." Hamilton believed in popular government but also believed that the entrenched local interests of state legislators hampered the public good and the true interests of the people. "The inquiry constantly is what will *please*, not what will *benefit* the people. In such a government there can be nothing but temporary expedient, fickleness, and folly." He grew more cynical about the prospects of his country. "The more I see, the more I find reason for those who love this country to weep over its blindness."

For all his complaints about the weakness of Congress and his need to focus on establishing a career, Hamilton was elected to Congress in July. "I am now a grave counsellor-at-law, and shall soon be a grave member of Congress," he wrote to Lafayette. He was condemned to "run the race of ambition" his entire life. The burden of responsibility to help turn public affairs around drew Hamilton to Congress, which began its session in late November.

In the meantime, Hamilton received the terrible news that his beloved friend, John Laurens, had been killed in a skirmish. The pair had exchanged some letters in midsummer reflecting on the duties of statesmanship now that the war for independence was winding down and goal of independence nearly won. Laurens had wished to see his friend "fill only the first offices of the republic." In turn, Hamilton encouraged Laurens to end his military service and serve in Congress. "Quit your sword my friend, put on the toga, come to Congress. We know each other's sentiments, our views are the same. We have fought side by side to make America free. Let us hand in hand struggle to make her happy." Then, in late August, all the potential for greatness Laurens exhibited came to a tragic end. The inconsolable Hamilton informed Lafayette: "Poor Laurens, he has fallen a sacrifice to his ardor in a trifling skirmish in South Carolina. You know how truly I loved him and will judge how much I regret him."

In Philadelphia, Hamilton struck up a friendship with another nationalist-minded politician, James Madison of Virginia. The growing circle of nationalists included Robert and Gouverneur Morris. The nationalists were bound by a common goal of a stronger national government rather than the ineffectual confederation. Indeed, Rhode Island continually frustrated the ability of Congress to pass an impost, or 5 percent tax on imports, for revenue since the states generally failed to meet the congressional tax requisitions. Hamilton and Madison sat on a committee that tried to deal with the intransigent state. "The truth is that no federal constitution can exist without powers that, in their exercise, affect the internal policy of the component members." Then, even more devastating news arrived. Only a month after Hamilton had taken his seat in Philadelphia, Congress received word that Virginia had rescinded its earlier approval of the impost, which was now obviously dead.

With an ominous sense of timing, in late December, a three-man officer delegation including Hamilton's friend, General Alexander McDougall, arrived in Philadelphia with a petition to Congress. The officers were irate because they had not been paid in months, and in some cases, years. General Washington took note of their discontent at winter quarters in Newburgh, New York. "The temper of the army has become more irritable than at any period since the commencement of the war." He feared that "a train of evils will follow of a very serious and distressing nature" that could spell trouble for the republican civil government.

The officers met with Robert Morris. We do not know what was discussed, but comments of the participants and events seem to bear out that a group of nationalists including Hamilton, Robert Morris, and Gouverneur Morris joined efforts with the officers to pressure Congress to assume greater powers. On January 6, 1783, the officers met with the Congress and hinted at a possible mutiny. They laid their threatening petition before the shocked members of Congress. "We have borne all that man can bear—our property is expended—our private resources are at an end, and our friends are wearied out and disgusted with our incessant applications." The officers had served honorably and at great personal sacrifice, and they expected that Congress would meet its obligations for a just compensation. If Congress did not act, the petition cautioned, "any further experiments on their patience may have fatal consequences." When questioned by members of Congress about the danger of a mutiny, one of the delegation replied with a chilling answer. "The temper of the army was such that they did not reason or deliberate coolly on consequences, and therefore a disappointment might throw them blindly into extremities."

Congress considered this great threat to the civilian government. The delegates were not reassured when financier Morris informed them that there was no money available to pay the army until the impost was passed. The members knew the impost had no chance of passing. They settled for weakly appointing Hamilton and others to a committee to deliberate on the petition. After weeks of fumbling, Congress promised to find the revenue to pay the salaries and a lump-sum pension, but it was voted down. During the debate, Hamilton railed against the present revenue system. He stated that it was "a vicious system of collection prevailed." He admitted that it "expedient to introduce the influence of officers . . . [who were] interested in supporting the power of Congress."

Pressure mounted on Congress to resolve the issue when news of the preliminary peace treaty with Great Britain arrived from Paris in early February. The soldiers feared that Congress would disband the army rather than pay them. The tense situation was on the verge of exploding.

Hamilton tried to persuade General Washington to join the nationalists supporting a funding system. Hamilton knew that the commander-in-chief's prestige would be an invaluable asset to persuade Congress. On February 13, he wrote to Washington surveying the temper of the army and the lack of decision in Congress. The conclusion was inescapable in Hamilton's mind. "It is probable we shall not take the proper measures, and if we do not a few months may open an embarrassing scene." Hamilton all but admitted he was pressuring Congress into assuming greater powers. "The claims of the army urged with moderation, but with firmness, may operate on those weak minds which are influenced by their apprehensions more than their judgments; so as to produce a concurrence in the measures which the exigencies of affairs demand. They may add weight to the applications of Congress to the several states." He acknowledged that it would be difficult to moderate a rebellious army, but then suggested that Washington might lend his prestige to the scheme and "guide the torrent, and bring order perhaps even good, out of confusion."

Hamilton's guiding motive was to preserve the national honor by meeting the country's obligations to its creditors and the patriots who shed their blood for American liberties. "The great desideratum at present is the establishment of general funds, which alone can do justice to the creditors of the United States (of whom the army forms the most meritorious class), restore public credit and supply the future wants of government."

While Washington shared Hamilton's frustrations, he would not take the bait. He was well acquainted with the suffering of the army and sympathetic to a more energetic national government. But Washington held fast to his trust that Congress and the states would do justice for the army. "The states cannot, surely, be so devoid of common sense, common honesty, and common policy as to refuse their aid." Washington recoiled at the thought of a mutiny against the civilian government. He was shaken that the war for American independence would end in "civil commotions" and "blood." He advised Hamilton, "Unhappy situation this! God forbid we should be involved in it."

On March 8, congressional inaction produced another warning from the officers in Newburgh. "Faith has its limits, as well as temper; and there are points beyond which neither can be stretched without sinking into cowardice, or plunging into credulity." Their fortunes and their sacred honor were at stake.

Washington wrote Hamilton a few days later and suspected that some members of Congress were scheming with the army. Washington averred that he had a responsibility to "arrest on the spot, the foot that stood wavering on a tremendous precipice; to prevent the officers from being taken by surprise while their passions were all inflamed, and to rescue them from plunging themselves into a gulf of civil horror from which there might be no receding." Washington sincerely hoped the members of Congress and his officers would act honorably and fulfill their sacred duties to the republican government.

On March 15, Washington entered the Temple of Virtue, the new assembly hall in the Newburgh camp, to address his officers. The general delivered a speech upbraiding the officers for its recent threats against Congress. "How inconsistent with the rules of propriety! How unmilitary! And how subversive of all order and discipline." Washington appealed to the men's patriotism, virtue, and honor. He encouraged the army to be patient and endure the sufferings until Congress acted. When his words fell flat before the irate assembly, Washington famously pulled out his glasses to read a letter and said, "Gentlemen, you will permit me to put on my spectacles, for I have not only grown gray, but almost blind, in the service of my country." The Newburgh Conspiracy collapsed with Washington's dramatic gesture, though Congress never did honor its soldiers and disbanded the army in a few months.

Hamilton and Washington discussed the Newburgh Conspiracy in the aftermath. Hamilton asserted that, "If no excesses take place I shall not be sorry that ill-humors have appeared. I shall not regret importunity, if temperate, from the army." He was unapologetic and did not regret his role in the affair. He admitted that he thought "the discontents of the army might be turned to a good account. I am still of opinion that their earnest, but respectful applications for redress will still have a good effect." He believed that only drastic action could save the feeble union. Hamilton was willing to risk a military overthrow of the government to save the national union and honor. To do otherwise was a cowardly dereliction of duty as a statesman and patriot.

Washington responded in a measured way that sympathized with Hamilton's concerns for the new nation. He agreed that the sovereign states weakened the nation and made it an object for the predatory European powers. A greater continental perspective would create a unified national character, a revised constitution, and a sound national government. Nevertheless, the Newburgh Conspiracy was the wrong answer. "The idea of redress by force is too chimerical to have had a place in the imagination of any serious mind." Washington cautioned that, "The army is a dangerous instrument to play with."

CHAPTER 8

HAMILTON AND THE PRINCIPLE OF JUSTICE IN THE 1780S

Hamilton was drawn to the familiar surroundings of cosmopolitan, commercial New York, where he settled on Wall Street immediately upon the British withdrawal. He set up his law practice at 57 Wall Street and took on some controversial and unpopular cases that could have been detrimental to his fledgling career. He defended the rule of law and justice when he represented numerous Tories whose property had been confiscated. The question was connected to the national honor of the new nation because it was an obligation of the peace treaty. More importantly, he wanted to do what was right.

In November 1783, some thirty thousand Tories boarded British ships as they departed from New York. Hamilton thought the flight of so "large a number of valuable citizens" would negatively impact the state and the country. Moreover, Hamilton had always defended reason over the passions of the mob. "Our state will feel for twenty years at least the effects of the popular frenzy," because of the loss of many wealthy merchants and skilled artisans who were the backbone of a commercial economy. The New York legislature had passed a series of highly popular laws that violated the rights of the hated Tories. Hamilton confided to Gouverneur Morris that, "I will in the lump, tell you that we are doing those things which we ought not to do. Instead of wholesale regulations for the improvement of our polity and commerce, we are laboring to contrive methods to mortify and punish Tories and to explain away treaties."

Democratic majorities confiscated Tory estates, violating property rights wholesale. The 1779 Confiscation Act provided for the seizure and sale of Tory property. In 1782, the assembly passed the Citation Act, which banned Tories from collecting debts. Recently, in March 1783, the Trespass Act stipulated that citizens whose property had been occupied while the British garrisoned New York could sue the occupants for damages. Hamilton joked that he could earn a bonanza in legal fees because of the lawsuits. He told Morris tongue-in-cheek that, "legislative folly has afforded so plentiful a harvest to us lawyers that we have scarcely a moment to spare from . . . reaping." But his caseload reflected how many people were being treated unjustly and how seriously he took the issue.

In January 1784, Hamilton wrote the *Letter from Phocion* to address the controversy under the pseudonym of an Athenian general known for his magnanimity over defeated enemies. He crafted several arguments to attack the injustice of the laws and the illegality of the confiscations. The tyranny of the democratic majority driven by their passions to trample on the rights of a despised minority resulted in the unconstitutional laws. The laws broke the 1783 peace treaty with Great Britain and sullied the national honor because "they advise us to become the scorn of nations, by violating the solemn engagements of the United States." The state was violating the laws of nations and contradicting the right of the sovereign nation to conduct foreign affairs through Congress. This dangerous precedent would allow state sovereignty to trump national power. "Would not all the powers of the confederation be annihilated and the union dissolved?" More-over, it would invite British retribution by not complying with the terms of the treaty. The laws also violated the right of trial by jury, which was the dictate of "natural justice, and a fundamental princi-ple of law and liberty." They violated the natural rights principles of "equal justice" and the "true principles of universal liberty." Hamilton defended the Whig principles animating the American Revolution, which he asserted "cherishes legal liberty, holds the rights of every individual sacred, condemns or punishes no man without regular trial." Departing from these principles would "corrupt the principles of our government, and furnish precedents for future usurpations on the rights of the community."

After excoriating the anti-Tory laws, Hamilton accepted cases helping Tories sue to recover their lost property. It was a risky move for his legal practice and his reputation to be acting as counsel for such unpopular persons and an unpopular cause, but it was a matter of justice. Elizabeth Rutgers was Hamilton's most famous client whose case was an important test of the law. She was an elderly widow who had owned an alehouse and brewery before the British occupation of New York in 1776. After she fled and abandoned her business, two British merchants operated the brewery for the duration of the war. Benjamin Waddington and his business partner paid no rent to the American owner, but they did make improvements to the property. The structure was consumed in a fire only a few days before the British departed in late 1783. Mrs. Rutgers sought £8,000 in damages from Waddington under the Trespass Act.

On June 29, 1784, Hamilton made his case before the Mayor's Court of New York City. First, he argued that the Trespass Act violated the law of nations that allowed Waddington to run the brewery. Second, Hamilton contended that the Trespass Act was void because it conflicted with the peace treaty made by the Confederation Congress and was therefore binding upon the individual states. Third, this was therefore an argument for the court's power of judicial review to invalidate a state law that conflicted with a national one or a law that grossly impinged upon the individual property rights of a minority group.

The court issued its opinion in mid-August and generally rejected Hamilton's arguments. The court neither invalidated the Trespass Act nor did it award Mrs. Rutgers full damages as compensation. The widowed alehouse owner did win damages of £800 for the use of her property when the defendant failed to pay rent for two years under the law of nations. Still, the New York press and legislature censured the decision because they considered it favorable to Tories. The assembly asserted that the court had "subverted all law and good order," and Hamilton came in for some abuse. Nevertheless, he courageously persevered in his efforts to win justice for the Tories and would take on nearly seventy cases over the next few years.

The anti-Tory legislation in New York embroiled Hamilton in another public controversy while he was preparing the *Rutgers* case. New York landed gentleman and manor lord Robert Livingston had opposed the Tory laws until he hit upon a scheme to buy up their confiscated property cheaply. However, much of his wealth was not liquid because it was tied up in his existing property holdings. Therefore, on February 17, 1784, Livingston and other speculators petitioned the assembly for a land bank that would lend money to borrowers secured by real estate. Hamilton opposed the land bank because he thought that the supporters were improperly and dishonorably using the bank to enrich themselves. His own interests were at stake because his brother-in-law, John Church, and his partner, Jeremiah Wadsworth, were attempting to organize their own Bank of New York. The battle triggered a dispute between the upstate landed elite and the commercial interests in New York City, which mirrored the political struggle between the localists and nationalists.

Hamilton and several business leaders gathered at the Merchant's Coffee House only a week later to elect a board and draft an organizing charter for the bank. They selected General Alexander McDougall as the bank's chairman and Hamilton as a director. Based upon his experience studying banking during the war with Robert Morris, who organized the Bank of Philadelphia, Hamilton drew up the charter for its New York counterpart. While Governor George Clinton and Livingston defeated the chartering of the Bank of New York in the assembly, Hamilton and his allies also blocked the land bank. The Bank of New York opened its doors a few months later as a private bank and would not secure a charter until after the Constitution was ratified.

Justice for slaves was another issue in New York that commanded Hamilton's attention in the mid-1780s. Hamilton had developed a strong aversion to slavery growing up in the West Indies, where he witnessed the horrors of the Atlantic slave trade and slaves working under brutal conditions. His participation in John Laurens's visionary emancipation plan during the war was an early example of his work for the abolition of slavery. The 1783 Peace Treaty had included a provision for the return of runaway slaves who had joined with the British. Hamilton would later comment that this clause violated principles of natural justice and humanity. "In the interpretations of treaties, thing *odious* or *immoral* are not to be presumed. The abandonment of negroes, who had been induced to quit their masters . . . promising them liberty, to fall again under the yoke of their masters and into slavery is as *odious* and *immoral* a thing as can be conceived. It is odious not only as it imposes an act of perfidy on one of the contracting parties, but as it tends to bring back to servitude men once made free."

In early February 1785, Hamilton attended one of the first meetings of the New York Society for Promoting the Manumission of Slaves with John Jay, Robert Troup, Alexander McDougall, and other friends. The group was animated by the universal principles of natural rights equality and liberty from the American Revolution. One of their statements asserted the ideal of the Declaration of Independence that all humans were created equal. "The benevolent creator and father of men, having given to them all an equal right to life, liberty, and property, no sovereign power on earth can justly deprive them of either."

The New York Manumission Society engaged in various educational activities to enlighten the public on the evils of slavery and the tragic episodes of free blacks in the state being forced back into slavery. It engaged in advocacy and lobbying in the state legislature when it pressed for gradual emancipation schemes, one of which was adopted. The society even set up an African Free School for the education of young slaves in manufacturing trades and domestic arts. While perhaps not the main public concern in his mind, Hamilton was dedicated to the abolition of slavery.

Hamilton was active in the emancipation society. He served on a committee that pressed fellow members to emancipate their slaves according to various timetables depending on the age of the slaves. The members of the society pushed back against the proposal and kept emancipation a matter of voluntary participation. He joined the society in petitioning the assembly to halt the exportation of slaves out of the states to potentially more horrifying conditions and then to end the slave trade in New York. Hamilton affixed his name to one of the petitions that labeled the slave trade as "so repugnant to humanity and so inconsistent with the liberality and justice which should distinguish a free and enlightened people." The national honor of a natural rights republic demanded working toward the realization of the universal equality, consent, and rights of all people.

Another public controversy consumed Hamilton's attention in the mid-1780s. Many ordinary citizens and important statesmen such as Thomas Jefferson, Benjamin Franklin, and Samuel and John Adams were concerned about the Society of Cincinnati, which was a fraternal organization of Continental Army officers with hereditary membership. The Society of Cincinnati struck these opponents as a dangerous agent of antidemocratic aristocracy and a potential seedbed of a standing army in the new republic. George Washington was so concerned that he urged the first national meeting of the society to end the hereditary character of the organization. Although the general thought the reaction was exaggerated and misapprehended the purpose of the society, he pleaded with state chapters to adopt this prudent alteration. Washington told his former aide that the society must change "if the Society of Cincinnati mean to live in peace with the rest of their fellow citizens." Washington was highly sensitive to avoid disunity and promote harmony in American society.

Hamilton was more interested in leaping to defend the honor of the society and its members. In a July 1786 speech to his New York chapter, Hamilton averred, "To heaven and our own bosoms, we recur for vindication from any misrepresentations of our intentions." Since the charges against the organization were false, he told his fellow Cincinnati the society must resist the pressure to change. He warned the society that it must keep hereditary membership or risk dying out after the present generation. Yet he suggested a change to the rule of admitting only the firstborn (primogeniture) in membership because "it refers to birth what ought to belong to merit only, a principle inconsistent with the genius of a society founded on friendship and patriotism." He was just as quick to leap to the defense of the national Union and proposals to strengthen it during the decade.

CHAPTER 9

HAMILTON AND THE NATIONAL UNION IN THE 1780S

While Hamilton was strongly dedicated to the emancipation of slaves and the Society of Cincinnati, there were more pressing political questions that needed answers if the new nation was to survive. He devoted much of his energy to revising the Articles of Confederation before the government collapsed. At the end of the war, he had written, "We have now happily concluded the great work of independence but much remains to be done to reach the fruits of it. Our prospects are not flattering. Every day proves the inefficacy of the present confederation."

Hamilton blamed the sovereign states for not relinquishing any of their powers to the national government since the end of the war. He saw firsthand the consequences of localism of New York governor George Clinton as the two sides waged political battles. Congress could still not raise revenue or pass taxes on imports. A severe postwar depression in New York and the other states caused falling prices for goods and trade. Farmers were deeply in debt and plagued by heavy state taxes. Credit and money were scarce, but discontent was rife. States passed tariffs on each other and engaged in trade wars, and almost went to war with each other. For example, New York assumed national powers by passing tariffs on British goods from the West Indies and on goods from New Jersey and Connecticut. Meanwhile, the national government had a one-house Congress with no effectual executive or court system, and thus lacked basic principles of separation of powers and checks and balances. Certain laws and amendments to the Articles demanded supermajorities or unanimity. The urgent problems of the Confederation increasingly commanded Hamilton's attention.

In late March 1785, representatives from Maryland and Virginia met at the Mount Vernon home of nationalist George Washington. Over several days, the commissioners hammered out an agreement to resolve several trade and navigation disputes. The meeting was a model of interstate cooperation among continentally minded individuals to resolve disputes and discuss strengthening the national government. Washington's thinking about the Articles of Confederation and national honor mirrored Hamilton's own. If the power of the states continued to thwart the national government, then it would "sap the constitution of these states (already too weak)—destroy our national character—and render us contemptible in the eyes of Europe."

Hamilton won election to the New York Assembly in April 1786. "The derangement of our public affairs by the feebleness of the general confederation drew me again reluctantly into public life." Several nationalists wanted to build on the experience of the Mount Vernon Conference. In late 1785, Virginian James Madison pushed for a "general meeting of commissioners from the states to consider and recommend a federal plan for regulating commerce." The following spring, the Virginia Assembly called for a general meeting of the states to build a uniform system of commercial regulation. Hamilton was very pleased at the direction of the nationalist movement and seized the opportunity to achieve his goal of strengthening the national government to build an enduring republic.

In May 1786, the New York Assembly voted Hamilton one of the six commissioners to attend the Annapolis Convention. He and his fellow delegates were authorized to examine American commerce and develop a uniform system to recommend. Hamilton traveled to Annapolis in early September and formed a strong alliance with Madison, who shared Hamilton's sense of desperation. They would form a political alliance over the next three years that would bear great fruit in creating a more perfect Union.

Madison developed a habit of preparing for political conventions through months of voracious reading in history and philosophy to hone his thinking. For Annapolis, he read crates full of books that Thomas Jefferson shipped from Paris. Madison formulated his thoughts into a study, "Notes on Ancient and Modern Confederacies," that examined the general tendency of confederacies to have weak central governments in favor of stronger local authorities. The lesson of history to Madison was clear that these weak confederacies were fatally flawed by their disunity that led to disintegration. Madison and Hamilton had had plenty of practical experience with the problems of the American confederation during their time in Congress, and Hamilton's service in the army had confirmed their voluminous reading. The like-minded pair met at Mann's Tavern in Annapolis and spoke about their ideas and strategy for hours while they waited for the other delegates. They were prepared to tackle much larger political issues than economic harmony among the states.

Their optimism for the Annapolis Convention was dashed when so few delegates arrived. On Friday, September 8, Madison anxiously predicted that they would not even be able to assemble a quorum. "The prospect of a sufficient number to make the meeting respectable is not flattering," he wrote. Madison and Hamilton lamented how the meeting symbolized the ailing confederation. By Monday, only twelve commissioners from five states met in the Maryland State House and elected John Dickinson chairman. With great frustration, it was obvious to the gathered individuals that they could not proceed with the planned business. They settled for drafting a report to the states.

Virginian Edmund Randolph began writing the message when Hamilton nudged Randolph out and took over the assignment. The New Yorker wanted to make sure that the report was sufficiently strong and did not equivocate with the states. When he delivered a resolution that was too extreme even for the assembled group, Madison privately urged Hamilton to moderate his stance and language. "You had better yield to this man for otherwise all Virginia will be against you," Madison advised. Hamilton conceded the point, which he rarely did, and toned down the report following Madison's conciliatory advice.

On September 14, the commissioners unanimously agreed to the final report they would send to the states. "That there are important defects in the system of the federal government is acknowledged by the acts of all those states, which have concurred in the present meeting," it read. Hamilton's concern for the national honor and durability of the national government survived in the report. The "greater and more numerous" defects of the national Union caused great "embarrassments which characterize the present state of our national affairs—foreign and domestic." They recommended another convention to deliberate candidly about national state of affairs and seek effectual remedies. They recommended that that states send representatives to a Philadelphia convention the following May to "render the constitution of the federal government adequate to the exigencies of the Union." The delegates submitted it to Congress, where it would languish in committee, and returned to their respective states, where they would lead the fight for a constitutional convention.

The call for a convention might have gone largely ignored except for a group of concerned nationalists but for the eruption of Shays' Rebellion in late 1786 in western Massachusetts and surrounding states. Angry farmers rebelled against crushing taxes that they could not pay because of depressed prices and heavy debts. When no relief was forthcoming, the angry farmers assembled into armed mobs that closed several courthouses throughout the state to prevent foreclosure proceedings. The national government was powerless to suppress the insurrection. Finally, Massachusetts governor James Bowdoin defeated the rebels with a private subscription army of forty-four hundred men funded by merchants.

The episode starkly demonstrated the weakness of the national government in the face of a domestic rebellion. It provided the impetus for the nationalists to advocate for a stronger government. Madison thought that the insurrection gave "new proofs of the necessity of such a vigor in the general government as will be able to restore health to any diseased part of the federal constitution." Hamilton was curiously quiet about Shays' Rebellion especially since he was a keen observer of public affairs and profoundly wedded to the idea of strengthening the national government. The silence is probably best explained by the fact that Hamilton was a long-standing opponent of lawless mob rule and a well-known supporter of revising the Articles. The crisis confirmed his thinking and required little comment. In late February 1787, the nationalists appealed to Congress, which approved the Annapolis resolution for the Philadelphia Convention to revise the Articles.

That same month, Hamilton struggled valiantly against the Clintonian forces for New York's ratification of the 5 percent national impost. He warned the assembly that the confederation was tearing itself apart at the seams and inviting internal collapse or foreign invasion. "If these states are not united under a federal government, they will infallibly have wars with each other and their divisions will subject them to all the mischiefs of foreign influence and intrigue," he said. Hamilton was frustrated but not surprised when the impost failed yet again.

Hamilton was more pleased that the assembly agreed to his motion to send delegates to the upcoming Philadelphia Convention. He proposed to send five delegates, but was again disappointed by the power of the Clintonians to frustrate his national designs. They reduced the number of delegates to three and added two localists, John Lansing Jr. and Robert Yates, to box Hamilton in at every corner and frustrate his plan. Hamilton knew that he would make a limited contribution to the convention months before it convened in Philadelphia. The transparent moves on the part of the Clintonians were clear to any observer. Madison was serving in Congress and noted that the pair were "pretty much linked to the antifederal party here, and are likely of course to be a clog on their colleague."

CHAPTER 10

THE CONSTITUTIONAL CONVENTION

In early May, members of the Virginia delegation began arriving in Philadelphia for the convention. The convention was unable to reach a quorum as planned on May 14 as delegates traveled to the city from distant states. However, Hamilton would have been pleased to learn that the nationalists from Virginia (including his nationalist-minded colleagues, Madison and Washington) were meeting with the Pennsylvanians for hours at a time to discuss strategy. Madison had followed his usual pattern of intense preparation for the convention. He had produced a list of the "Vices of the Political System" that served as a basis for his Virginia Plan with its stronger national government. The Virginians and Pennsylvanians planned to introduce Madison's handiwork early in the convention to control the direction of the convention.

On May 18, Hamilton arrived in Philadelphia with Yates and stayed at the Indian Queen Tavern. He engaged in preliminary discussions at the state house and the informal talk in the public houses where the delegates gathered for meals and drinks. He had the opportunity to restore his former warm ties to Washington and joined in the strategic planning with other nationalists. The delegates assembled at the state house a week later for the beginning of the convention.

The members of the Constitutional Convention spent the first day deciding rules of order and procedures that grounded the deliberations in civility. Washington was unanimously elected, which lent an air of gravity and legitimacy to the proceedings. Hamilton nominated Major William Jackson to be secretary. When the delegates selected a Rules Committee, they chose Hamilton along with George Wythe and Charles Pinckney. The convention then adjourned until Monday when the Rules Committee would submit their recommendations.

After a long weekend, Hamilton and the other members of the Rules Committee offered their proposals. Hamilton had wanted the individual delegates each to have one vote because he knew that voting by delegation would allow Yates and Lansing to negate every vote he took on the convention floor. However, the delegates agreed with the majority of the Rules Committee that each state would have one vote, following the procedure of the Continental Congress and Confederation Congress. The convention also resolved to conduct their sessions in secret. This would allow for greater frankness in deliberations and allow delegates to change their minds during debate free from public scrutiny. Hamilton later explained, "Had the deliberations been open while going on, the clamors of faction would have prevented any satisfactory result. Had they been afterwards disclosed, much food would have been afforded to inflammatory declamation." The delegates also resolved to treat each other with civility, a rule that would be tested as debates became heated that summer.

Georgian William Pierce left penetrating portraits of the delegates' debating styles and characters. Hamilton was a keen, analytical thinker and persuasive orator in Pierce's opinion. But Pierce noted that Hamilton had an arrogant air about him that might turn off his fellow delegates. "Col. Hamilton is deservedly celebrated for his talents. He is a practitioner of the law, and reputed to be a fine scholar. To a clear and strong judgment he unites the ornaments of fancy . . . he enquires into every part of his subject with the searchings of philosophy, and when he comes forward he comes highly charged with interesting matter, there is no skimming over the surface of a subject with him. He must sink to the bottom to see what foundation it rests on. . . . His manners are tinctured with stiffness and sometimes with a degree of vanity that is highly disagreeable."

On Tuesday, May 29, Virginian Edmund Randolph introduced the Virginia Plan. The plan included the nationalist thinking that had guided Madison and greatly strengthened the national government from what it had been under the Articles. Central to the plan was a veto by the national government over state laws.

Hamilton generally liked what he heard, though the plan did not go far enough in strengthening national powers at the expense of the states. The debate became heated almost immediately, and sparks flew within the New York delegation. He averred that the plan rightly inquired "whether the United States were susceptible of one government, or required a separate existence connected only by leagues offensive and defensive and treaties of commerce." Yates took exception to the obvious nationalist aims of the plan. Yates had attended the convention deeply suspicious of the intentions of the nationalists, and the Virginia Plan had confirmed his fears. He thought he detected a design to create "a strong consolidated union in which the idea of states should be nearly annihilated." The next day, Yates even opposed the principle of separation of powers when he voted no on a proposal that the national government "ought to be established consisting of a supreme legislature, executive, and judiciary." Hamilton got a taste of the trouble he would face when Lansing arrived in Philadelphia.

On June 1, the convention considered the executive branch of government. The revolutionary experience of tyranny under the British king had led them to create weak governors, and there was no independent executive under the Articles of Confederation. The convention deadlocked over the basic question of whether there would be a single executive or a council. Hamilton supported Pennsylvanian James Wilson's proposal for a single executive because it would imbue the office with "energy, dispatch, and responsibility." Others responded that this was a recipe for monarchy. When Franklin suggested that the executive should be a model of disinterested republicanism by serving the public without a salary, Hamilton seconded the motion, which he thought a "respectable," honorable idea. He also supported a motion "to give the executive an absolute negative on the laws" as a check on the national legislature, citing the example of the king of England. However, John Lansing arrived and took his seat in the convention during the debate on the executive. Consequently, on June 4, the New York delegation voted no on creating a single executive. Hamilton must have sat there fuming. He would be outvoted every time.

On Friday, June 15, matters became even worse when New Jersey delegate William Paterson rose and offered the New Jersey Plan as an alternative to the Virginia Plan. This plan simply revised the Articles and kept the locus of power firmly within the sovereign states. The Congress would be empowered to regulate interstate trade and to tax. Lansing rose in support of the plan because it "sustains the sovereignty of the respective states." He warned the advocates of the Virginia Plan that, "The states will never sacrifice their essential rights to a national government." Yates scribbled down a few notes during the convention and recorded that day, "Col. Hamilton cannot say he is in sentiment with either plan." The Virginia Plan did not propose a government that was strong enough, and the New Jersey Plan merely revised the failed confederation. Hamilton had heard enough. He characteristically plunged into his work and spent the entire weekend at his writing desk formulating a third framework of government that would comport with his political philosophy.

On Monday, June 18, Hamilton rose and delivered a marathon six-hour speech that left the delegates speechless. He stated he had not spoken much because of the "delicate situation with respect to his state." He offered a third plan that would better secure "the public safety and happiness." He even praised the British government because it provided the United States with a model of balance between "public strength with individual security."

The plan of government had a strong national government. Hamilton asserted that the national government must have a "complete sovereignty" that "must swallow up the state powers." The national government would have a bicameral Congress with Senators elected for life (and good behavior) modeled after the "most noble institution" of the House of Lords. The House of Representatives was a highly democratic house of Congress in his plan. The executive would also be elected to serve for life and good behavior based upon the British monarch, which was the "only good one on the subject." He asserted that the government he proposed was still republican because "all the magistrates are appointed, and vacancies are filled, by the people, or a process of election originating with the people." Moreover, he argued the executive and senate would not be centers of corruption (as many delegates and later Anti-Federalists feared) because they would not have to seek office or dispense favors. The national government was limited by the principles of separation of powers and checks and balances that were sorely lacking in the Articles of Confederation. Hamilton thought his framework of government would achieve the requisite "stability and permanence."

Hamilton admitted that he was "aware that it went beyond the ideas of most members," but he thought that the American people had experienced a crisis of governance that made them "ready to go as far at least as he proposes." Public opinion was probably not ready for such a radical plan of government. The delegates certainly were shocked by the speech and adjourned without comment.

The reasons for Hamilton's speech are unclear and still debated today. Ron Chernow calls the speech "daft" and "hare-brained" because it was so at odds with the political thinking of the delegates and effectively ruined whatever influence Hamilton had on the floor of the convention. Moreover, the speech haunted him for a decade and gave his enemies plenty of ammunition in labeling him a monarchist. On the other hand, other scholars contend that Hamilton was expressing honest political opinions he thought necessary to solve the great political crises of the 1780s. Moreover, they argue that Hamilton might have had proposed such a radical plan that would make the Virginia Plan seem more moderate and break the deadlock in the convention over the rival plans. Hamilton was a brilliant political thinker and strategist, and this strategic ploy was hardly beyond his abilities.[1]

The debate the following day gave Hamilton an opportunity to clarify his position. James Wilson reassured the delegates he "did not mean one that would swallow up the state governments as seemed to be wished by some gentlemen . . . contrary to the opinion of Col. Hamilton that they might not only subsist but subsist on friendly terms with the former." Hamilton rose to his own defense. He stated that the national legislature "must . . . have indefinite authority. . . . As states, he thought they ought to be abolished. But he admitted the necessity of leaving in them, subordinate jurisdictions." Hamilton argued that a stronger Union would actually protect smaller states. "The more close the Union of the states, and the more complete the authority of the whole; the less opportunity will be allowed the stronger states to injure the weaker," he explained. A few days later, he argued against the federal principle when he opposed state legislatures electing national representatives. Keeping a constant vigil on state sovereignty "could not be too watchfully guarded against" in his opinion.

By the end of June, the convention was still deadlocked over the shape and powers of the national legislature with no resolution in sight. Benjamin Franklin tried to break the impasse by suggesting that prayers might contribute to a spirit of compromise. Hamilton opposed the proposal because he thought welcoming a minister in for prayer might invite speculation among the public about the state of the convention. Prayer would have been welcome "at the beginning of the convention" but not in the middle of deliberations. A false myth has circulated that Hamilton impiously asserted that the convention did not need "foreign aid."

In the coming weeks, a Committee of Eleven settled the dispute, creating a national Congress with a House of Representatives based upon popular representation and a Senate based upon state equality. Once they resolved the Congress, the delegates then returned to a discussion of the executive branch but reached no firm conclusions. Hamilton, however, was absent for the debates. On June 30, he left the convention because he was frustrated with his impotence and wanted to return to his private business. George Mason noted that "Yates and Lansing never voted in one single instance with Hamilton, who was so much mortified at it that he went home."

Curiously, Hamilton wrote Washington and explained that the United States faced a decisive tipping point. The people were ready for a stronger central government, and the crisis demanded it. He explained he had "taken particular pains to discover the public sentiment and I am more and more convinced that this is the critical opportunity for establishing the prosperity of this country on a solid foundation." He thought he sensed that there was "an astonishing revolution for the better in the minds of the people . . . that a strong well-mounted government will better suit the popular palate than one of a different complexion." He confessed to Washington that he had abandoned the convention out of frustration. "I own to you sir that I am seriously and deeply distressed at the aspect of the councils which prevailed when I left Philadelphia. I fear that we shall let slip the golden opportunity of rescuing the American empire from disunion, anarchy, and misery."

He promised to return, but only "if I have reason to believe that my attendance at Philadelphia will not be mere waste of time."

On July 6, Yates and Lansing left the convention for good for the contrary reason that it was creating a powerful central government. The New York delegation collapsed and was no longer represented in the convention. Even if Hamilton did return, the delegation could not continue with a single member. He appealed to the two men to return "for the sake of propriety and public opinion" and offered to accompany them, but they refused. Hamilton blamed the influence of Governor Clinton because he had "clearly betrayed an intention to excite prejudices beforehand against whatever plan should be proposed by the Convention."

The convention proceeded in its deliberations without the benefit of Alexander Hamilton, or any New York delegate. On July 27, a committee of five members received the assignment to reconcile and organize the convention's work. On August 6, the Committee of Detail delivered its report to the convention, which served as the basis for further discussion to resolve outstanding issues. During the next month, the convention would agree to a single president and a national judiciary in separate branches of the federal government.

Hamilton returned to the convention by August 13, after an absence of more than five weeks, and joined a debate on immigration. The convention was considering imposing a residency requirement for immigrants running for congressional offices or an outright ban. Hamilton was personally stung by the discussion and opposed the nativist measures with Scotsman James Wilson. Hamilton envisioned an America based upon equal opportunity and merit. He also defended the practical benefits of immigration. "The advantage of encouraging foreigners is obvious. Persons in Europe of moderate fortunes will be fond of coming here, where they will be on a level with the first citizens. I move that the section be so altered as to require merely citizenship and inhabitancy."

Hamilton soon returned home again. His very spotty attendance at the Constitutional Convention was hardly consistent with his railings against the government. In addition, he was one of the most vocal partisans for a convention to revise the Articles. He missed an opportunity to help craft a more perfect Union even if he was hamstrung in his official capacity. In New York, he attended a meeting of the New York Manumission Society that wrote a petition to the convention for ending slavery.

The strong antifederal opinion in New York helped serve as evidence for the necessity of the delegates agreeing to send the Constitution to the representatives of the people in popular ratifying conventions rather than state legislatures. They sought to prevent the enemies from hindering ratification. The delegates expected the localists in New York and elsewhere who controlled state legislatures to lead the opposition to ratification.

Hamilton returned to the convention for its final proceedings, including signing the Constitution. He joined Washington, Franklin, and others encouraging three dissidents—George Mason, Edmund Randolph, and Elbridge Gerry—who had increasingly objected to the concentration of national power. On September 6, he told the delegates he "had been restrained from entering into the discussions by his dislike of the scheme of government in general; but as he meant to support the plan to be recommended, as better than nothing." It was a measure of the confidence and respect that the others had for Hamilton that they appointed him to a committee of style even though he had missed most of the convention. In the last remaining debates, contrary to the usual view of Hamilton as a monarchist, he defended "a numerous representation in the other branch of the legislature [the House of Representatives] should be established."

On September 17, most of the delegates signed the Constitution and left Philadelphia after dining together at the City Tavern. As he traveled home, Hamilton had some time to reflect on the new American government created by the Constitution. He was in a curious position regarding the Constitution, which he had relatively little influence in crafting and did not seem to like very much. Still, the Constitution would enjoy few greater advocates fighting for its ratification. He plunged into the effort of political strategy and dedicated his unusual energy to forming political alliances, writing at a blistering speed, and leading the public defense of a document that hopefully would build a lasting constitutional republic. The powerful opposition of the Clintonites in New York meant that Hamilton had his work cut out for him in the coming months.

CHAPTER 11

LEADING THE CHARGE FOR RATIFICATION

New York was a key battleground state in the ratification debate. The Constitution could not be considered legitimate if a large state such as New York refused to ratify. While the Federalists who supported the Constitution faced uphill battles against the AntiFederalist opponents of the Constitution in several states, nowhere would this struggle be more difficult than New York. The fight would demand the greatest perseverance and the most convincing articulation of constitutional political philosophy in this daunting challenge. Luckily for the Federalists, Alexander Hamilton was a formidable statesman and just the man to lead in such a contest.

Hamilton developed a threefold strategy in leading the charge for ratification of the Constitution. First, he plotted strategy and kept track of developments across the nation with allies Madison and Washington. Second, he wrote a series of essays in New York elucidating the structure and principles of the Constitution to answer the charges of its critics. Third, he fought against overwhelming odds to persuade the delegates to the New York Ratifying Convention to approve the document. All these efforts were crucial. Victory was not foreordained, and the fate of the republic hung in the balance.

The Constitution was sent to Congress in New York and faced its first hurdle. The AntiFederalists immediately sprang into action and circulated their objections to the Constitution. James Madison and other delegates from the Constitutional Convention rushed to Congress and persuaded that body to send the document to popular state ratifying conventions for consideration.

In New York, hostile AntiFederalists savaged Hamilton's character in the press. The first piece was a satirical poem that accused Hamilton of unsavory ambition and deceit. The second charged that Hamilton's meteoric rise and fame was the result of glomming himself on to Washington. "I have also known an upstart attorney palm himself upon a great and good man for a youth of extraordinary genius under the shadow of such patronage make himself at once known and respected." The allegations infuriated Hamilton, who was ever sensitive to slights against his honor. In the coming months, both sides would engage in the political art of character assassination.

In early October, the AntiFederalists also fired the first salvo in the public debate over ratification in the country's newspapers. An AntiFederal writer using the name of "Centinel" published the first of several essays in New York papers asserting that the Constitution would destroy the states, introduce an aristocracy to America, and end republican self-government. Madison informed Washington that the New York newspapers were teeming with "vehement and virulent calumniations of the proposed government."

Hamilton conceived of responding to Centinel and the AntiFederalists with a series of essays while he was traveling from Albany to New York. He invited several friends to join the effort and convinced John Jay and Madison to contribute essays. The *Federalist* essays penned under the name of Publius were meant primarily to influence the outcome of the debate in New York, a bastion of AntiFederalism. Hamilton also transmitted the essays to Federalists around the country who were coordinating their strategy and thinking. Finally, the Federalists wanted to sway popular opinion in a highly literate, deliberative republican society that read and debated the essays in coffeehouses, taverns, and other public spaces.

On October 27, the first *Federalist* essay appeared in the *New York Independent Journal*. Hamilton wrote that Americans faced a historic decision that would determine the fate of republican government there and around the world. "It has been frequently remarked, that it seems to have been reserved to the people of this country, by their conduct and example, to decide the important question, whether societies of men are really capable or not, of establishing good government from reflection and choice, or whether they are forever destined to depend, for their political constitutions, on accident and force." This statement of American exceptionalism postulated that Americans enjoyed a unique deliberative moment to create an experiment in liberty under ideal conditions.

The proposed Constitution enjoyed widespread support in New York City but was unpopular upstate. "The new Constitution is as popular in this city as it is possible for anything to be—and the prospect thus far is favorable to it throughout the state. But there is no saying what turn things may take when the full flood of official influence is let loose against it." Indeed, the opposition would only grow worse in the coming months. "The Constitution proposed has in this state warm friends and warm enemies. The first impressions everywhere are in its favor, but the artillery of its opponents makes some impression. The event cannot be foreseen."

By mid-January 1788, five states—Delaware, Pennsylvania, New Jersey, Georgia, and Connecticut—had ratified. The AntiFederalists began to demand "prior amendments" that would be submitted to a second convention before the new government was accepted. The Massachusetts Federalists faced a very close vote and were forced to promise "subsequent amendments" including a bill of rights after the Constitution was ratified. As a result, on February 6, the Federalists won a narrow vote in Massachusetts, which became the sixth state to ratify the Constitution.

The *Federalist* was a monumental achievement that was written at the frenetic pace of almost one thousand words daily. Madison noted that, "In the beginning it was the practice of the writers . . . to communicate each to the other, their respective papers before they were sent to the press." But they were just as overwhelmed by the torrent of words as the opposition, the printers, and readers to keep up. The authors answered specific criticisms of the AntiFederalists, explicated the framework and principles of the proposed government upon which it was constructed, and employed historical examples in these complex essays. Hamilton's Herculean task was compounded by maintaining his legal practice, taking a seat in the national Congress, witnessing the birth of his fourth child, and attending to a variety of other personal and professional responsibilities. He apologized for not writing his friend Gouverneur Morris more frequently but, "The truth is that I have been so overwhelmed in avocations of one kind or another that I have scarcely had a moment to spare a friend."

By the spring of 1788, the ratification process had enjoyed relatively easy success thus far. Maryland and South Carolina successfully ratified and brought the number of states to eight—one shy of ratification. Yet the Constitution still had to face its greatest trial in the coming months.

Hamilton readily understood that the Constitution could still fail and did everything he could to assure success. New York and Virginia had yet to hold their ratifying conventions and had strong Anti-Federalist opposition. Hamilton knew that these critical states were necessary for ratification if the new government was to be considered legitimate in the minds of the American people. A Union without these two states was unthinkable. In late March, he and Madison organized the first thirty-six *Federalist* essays into a logically coherent whole and published them in a single bound volume. They began sending them liberally to friends in the remaining states to influence the outcome. In early April, the pair published the last *Federalist* essay in newspapers, and a second collected volume appeared in book form in time for the Virginia and New York Conventions.

In late April, New York held elections for its ratifying convention, and the results were devastating for the Federalists. AntiFederalists outnumbered the Federalists by a staggering forty-eight to nineteen. Hamilton lamented, "I fear much that the issue has been against us." Clinton's forces would control the convention, and would presumably defeat the Constitution or force prior amendments. Indeed, historian Pauline Meier called Clinton "The number-one enemy for those who fought for the Constitution—the man who defined the meaning of 'antifederalist.'"[1] Hamilton searched for a winning strategy since the outcome seemed predetermined. Perhaps swaying public opinion to create a "favorable disposition in the citizens at large" might help pressure the AntiFederalists to reconsider their position. But he knew that he could "count little on overcoming opposition by reason." More likely, the ratification by the large state of Virginia would carry significant weight in pressuring New York AntiFederalists. "Our only chances will be the previous ratification by nine states, which may shake the firmness of [Clinton's] followers." Still, he girded himself for a great battle at the convention.

Hamilton was not leaving anything to chance in winning ratification in New York. He wrote Madison in Virginia and asked his collaborator to send news as soon as possible. Hamilton stayed in constant communication and offered to pay for an express rider to speed word to New York. He made the same arrangement with Henry Knox in Massachusetts to send word of New Hampshire's decision. After all, he predicted that "an eventual disunion and civil war" would result if he failed. When Hamilton and the New York delegation departed for Poughkeepsie with a rousing farewell from a large crowd in mid-June, he had still not heard about the results from Virginia and was not confident about his own chances. It would be a cruel twist of fate if his own commercial state of New York would be the decisive clog destroying the new government.

The New York Ratifying Convention opened on June 17 at the Poughkeepsie courthouse with the AntiFederalists overwhelmingly in the majority. However, on June 19, the Federalists won several procedural points that would help to tilt the odds in their favor. The delegates agreed to debate the proposed Constitution line-by-line. The author of the *Federalist* would consequently have a great advantage over his adversaries explaining and defending every clause of the document and its reasoning. Moreover, the delay would allow news from Virginia (and from New Hampshire, which was less decisive) to arrive in New York.

Hamilton eloquently defended American constitutional principles at the convention with the same quality of arguments he made in the *Federalist*. He started with the republican principle of consent and representation. "The true principle of a republic . . . that the people should choose whom they please to govern them." He supported a stronger central government that governed effectively and protected the natural rights of the people. The weak Articles of Confederation was the greater threat to liberty than an energetic one with adequate powers. A stronger Union was necessary to "perpetuate our liberties, as it is to make us respectable."

Hamilton promised various constitutional checks on the government from becoming too powerful. He argued for the principle of separation of powers and checks and balances to divide and limit power. "When we have given a proper balance to the different branches of administration and fixed representation upon pure and equal principles."

On June 24, Hamilton's rider brought news that New Hampshire became the ninth state to ratify the Constitution, which met the standard set by the document to become the law of the land. However, it would only achieve real legitimacy if Virginia and New York ratified. The AntiFederalists were unmoved by New Hampshire's ratification with Clinton promising that it would not have the "least effect" and another stating it was a "trifling occurrence." Hamilton was shrewd enough to realize that regardless of how brilliantly he explained the Constitution to the Poughkeepsie delegates, his rhetoric would probably fail to persuade enough delegates to win ratification. He urgently wrote Madison several dispatches begging for information from Virginia. On July 2, he told Madison that there was "more and more reason to believe that our conduct will be influenced by yours."

That same day, Hamilton enthusiastically received and read aloud a letter from a rider who finally brought the news he had been waiting for that Virginia had ratified the Constitution. If Hamilton thought that the resistance of the AntiFederalists would be quelled by the news or that the Constitution would now experience a smooth path to ratification, he was sorely mistaken. Two days later, a Fourth of July parade in Albany turned into a melee when a copy of the Constitution was burned and a violent clash resulted in one death and several injuries. Moreover, the AntiFederalists switched tactics to fight for conditional ratification with both structural amendments and a bill of rights as the fierce debate stretched over a couple of weeks. But Hamilton stood firm for unconditional ratification.

Finally, a dozen AntiFederalists jumped ship under the weight of events and conceded victory to the Federalists if they would promise to make subsequent amendments in the First Congress. Hamilton conceded and made a motion for "recommendatory and explanatory" amendments. He even curiously decided to help Lansing and Melancton Smith draft a circular letter to the states calling for another convention. A second convention called to rectify the errors of the first was one of Madison's greatest fears, but Hamilton was prudent enough to grant a small concession to win the larger goal of a constitutional Union. He calculated that the AntiFederalists would be too divided and weakened to mount much of an effort to convene another convention. On July 26, New York ratified the Constitution by the narrow margin of 30–27. North Carolina and Rhode Island would continue to hold out for a bill of rights, but with New York's ratification, the Constitution was now the supreme law of the land.

The citizens of New York City honored the unparalleled contribution of their favorite son, Alexander Hamilton, during their grand celebrations. The artisans of New York jubilantly paraded through the streets for days. Thousands of New Yorkers marched, calling for the city to be named after him and waving banners with odes to Hamilton. Sailmakers created a large banner with his likeness holding the Constitution. A thirty-foot ship christened the *Hamilton* "sailed" down Broadway pulled by horses and fired a salute to the Constitution and Union. Hamilton basked in the public adulation. He had won the fame and glory he wanted as a lawgiver.

Hamilton had argued for a stronger national government for over a decade in war and peace. During the ratification deliberations, Hamilton worked assiduously to win assent from the people and their representatives for the new framework of government. He had great hope that the new republican government would prove to be a more durable and lasting Union. The machinery of government would not run on its own, however; it needed great effort to breathe life into it and lay a proper foundation of constitutional principles. Although it was initially unclear what role Hamilton was going to play in the new government, no one doubted that Hamilton would serve. In the span of a little over fifteen years, the immigrant to America had risen dramatically through his merit and unrelenting effort to become one of the greatest founders of the more perfect Union. He would bring the same zeal and brilliance in implementing his plans for the greatness of the new republic.

CHAPTER 12

SECRETARY OF THE TREASURY

Alexander Hamilton envisioned a strong American nation that took its rightful place among the great European powers. The first essential element of achieving this goal was an energetic national government that fulfilled the purposes of a sovereign nation in domestic and foreign policy. Secondly, the economy had to be developed to unleash the creative energies of the people who would share in a broad-based prosperity. Thirdly, a nation with a strong political system and a prosperous economy would have a powerful military establishment to defend its interests and principles in a world of empire and war. These key ingredients would contribute to the success of the American experiment in liberty and self-government.

The partisan debate that took shape in the 1790s distorted Hamilton's principles and intentions for the country. The Jeffersonians feared centralized government and falsely accused Hamilton of supporting monarchy and aristocracy. He believed in an energetic government with a strong executive, but his goal was a well-governed constitutional republic that executed its powers and protected the liberties of the people.

Similarly, his opponents would tar Hamilton with the charge that he was building an economy that benefited the rich and powerful interests at the expense of the people. The Jeffersonians were greatly concerned with corruption characterized by speculators and bankers who enriched themselves with dishonest schemes and ill-gotten gains while plunging the country into debt. The fact that Hamilton purposefully modeled his economic plan on the British system did not help make his case more popular. Hamilton had a modern economic vision that few at the time understood properly if at all. He wanted to restore American credit, create a banking system with a sound currency and lending power, and build an integrated national economy with a strong manufacturing base and infrastructure system that would bind together the commercial, manufacturing, and agricultural interests of the country for the advantage of all. Private enterprise would be encouraged to thrive by a constitutional system with the rule of law, property protections, reasonable and equitable taxation, patent protections for inventions, and uniform bankruptcy laws.

Americans had a healthy distrust of standing armies and military establishments after their experience under the British. Although Hamilton was a war hero who sacrificed much while fighting the British, his Jeffersonian opponents thought they detected a plot to use a powerful standing army to impose a monarchical political system and corrupt economy. Hamilton thought that a proper military establishment would have an army and navy capable of defending American sovereignty and American national honor. Hamilton realistically faced the dangerous world of empire to protect the interests of the rising American empire.

Hamilton became the first secretary of the treasury and accomplished his greatest contribution to the founding of the United States. His patriotic service in the Revolutionary War and his leadership in securing the Constitution would have been enough to win him accolades as an important member of the founding generation of Americans, but they would almost pale in comparison with his role as treasury secretary. He was President George Washington's chief advisor during most of the first two administrations. The West Indian immigrant and the Virginian "Father of His Country" shared a common republican vision of American greatness and collaborated in deciding domestic and foreign policies that created a vigorous new nation.

Hamilton did not wait long before helping to oversee the administration of the new government. One of the first and most critical decisions was to convince Washington to become the nation's first president. He pressed Washington in several letters in the summer and fall of 1788. Hamilton made it clear that Washington must answer the unanimous call of his country to leave retirement and serve the republic again. Hamilton told Washington that "the success of the new government in its commencement may materially depend" on his participation and would "make an infinite difference in the respectability with which the government will begin its operations." Washington was the only person who could "sufficiently unite the public opinion or can give the requisite weight to the office in the commencement of the government." Washington was the indispensable man to building an enduring American republic.

Hamilton thought that Washington serving as the first president was so essential that he began his efforts at political engineering as a national power broker. He thought there was a defect in the Constitution in which the president and vice president were the first and second-place vote-getters in the electoral college. He greatly feared that a few Anti-Federalists might intrigue to upset the workings of the new government by withholding their votes from Washington and deliver them instead to Clinton or John Adams. Hamilton bore no particular animus toward Adams, but the damage that would be done if Washington were not to be selected president was too great a risk.

Hamilton remained involved in New York politics because the states played a significant role in the new federal republic, especially in shaping the Congress. Hamilton warred with his old nemesis, George Clinton, and supported Robert Yates for governor because Yates had become a firm supporter of the Constitution once ratified. The mutual recriminations that resulted were familiar to any observer. Hamilton accused Clinton of being a narrow-minded localist, and Clinton shot back that Hamilton was an ambitious tool of the aristocracy. Governor Clinton was nevertheless reelected. Hamilton stumbled again politically when he threw his weight behind his friend Rufus King for a Senate seat over Robert Livingston's choice of New York mayor James Duane. King won, as did Hamilton's father-in-law, Philip Schuyler. Hamilton had made another powerful opponent in Livingston in New York politics.

Hamilton was more pleased to learn that the electoral college had selected the first president of the United States. Sixty-nine electors met on February 4, 1789, and unanimously elected George Washington president. John Adams came in second in the voting and became the vice president.

On April 30, Washington was inaugurated at Federal Hall in the nation's capital of New York. Washington dressed in a plain, homespun brown suit as a symbol that he was a republican president rather than a monarch. He was humbly sworn into office by Chancellor Livingston in a dignified ceremony on a second-floor balcony before a large crowd of his fellow American citizens. After Washington took his oath of office, the assembled crowd cheered wildly, and church bells pealed throughout the city. The president delivered his inaugural address laying down republican principles to guide the American people and their government. He advocated following the "genuine maxims of an honest and magnanimous policy" for "public prosperity and felicity." Rather than make specific policy recommendations, Washington encouraged support for "the talents, the rectitude, and the patriotism, which adorn the characters selected to devise and adopt them." He promised that "the pre-eminence of free government be exemplified by all the attributes which can win the affections of its citizens and command the respect of the world." Hamilton and his wife attended the inaugural ball a few weeks later, and Eliza danced with the president.

Washington wanted to shape the office of the presidency with the right tone by establishing precedents on presidential decorum and behavior. As he told Catherine Macaulay Graham: "There is scarcely any part of my conduct which may not hereafter be drawn into precedent. All see, and most admire, the glare which hovers around the trappings of elevated office. To me, there is nothing in it, beyond the luster which may be reflected from its connection with a power of promoting human felicity." His instinct was to chart a course of republicanism, avoiding too much reserve and distance from the people while eschewing too much familiarity. He solicited guidance from trusted advisors such as Hamilton. In early May, Hamilton offered some recommendations regarding presidential etiquette. The primary object in Hamilton's view was to preserve the dignity of the office. He suggested striking a balance between a high tone and American growing sense of equality. He advised a presidential levee once a week to receive visitors for half an hour of light conversation. The second recommendation was a few annual state dinners with members of Congress, other government leaders, and foreign dignitaries to honor patriotic occasions. The final suggestion included regular dinners with small gatherings of American officials. Washington followed this advice, but was too aloof and uncomfortable with the levees, and soon discontinued them.

The Congress convened and created the first cabinet departments including treasury, war, and state. Representative James Madison argued for a system of checks and balances in the appointments. The president would appoint officials subject to the Senate's approval. The president would also retain the power of removal. New Jersey representative Elias Boudinot urged the members of the House to create a Treasury Department headed by a "public financier" to deal with pressing public financial problems. "It will be attended with the most dreadful consequences to let these affairs run into confusion and ruin," he warned. The proposal met with immediate resistance from some representatives who feared it would be the center of corrupt manipulations. Elbridge Gerry warned that, "The creation of a financier with all the splendor and powers of office" would have "innumerable opportunities for defrauding the revenue, without check or control." He thought a board of commissioners would be less susceptible to corruption than a single person. Madison weighed in and argued that a single secretary would exercise the requisite energy in office. Congress established the executive departments that summer, and they would all be headed by a single person.

The initial contention over the proposed Treasury Department was compounded by even greater disputations over the federal government's taxing power. Madison took the lead in Congress to raise revenue for the national government because of several trying years in the Confederation Congress. On April 9, he delivered a speech conflating a strong national Union with an adequate ability to raise revenue in the House of Representatives. He declared that "the union, having recovered from the state of imbecility that heretofore prevented a performance of its duty" now had to act with vigor. The trade being conducted by hundreds of ships right in New York harbor (and other ports around the country) would provide the tax revenue necessary to solve some of America's most pressing financial problems. "Every gentleman sees the prospect from our harvest from the spring importations is daily vanishing; and if [Congress] delay levying and collecting an impost there will be no importations of any consequence on which the law is to operate because, by that time all the spring vessels will have arrived and unloaded."

Madison proposed four bills with the dual purpose of raising revenue and protecting American industry and trade. The bills included a 5 percent tariff (or impost) on a variety of goods, a tonnage fee on all shipping importing goods (with much higher fees on foreign vessels), a customs collection system, and federal control of all lighthouses. Congressional debates caused a great deal of sectional conflict as North and South each pursued their own regional interests related to taxing certain items, and protecting their own industries and shipping.

Madison and many southerners wanted discriminatory tonnage fees against Great Britain for its imperial restrictions against the United States, particularly in Canada and the West Indies. They were disgruntled that Great Britain regulated American trade with the empire, while the United States imported almost 90 percent of their manufactured goods from Great Britain. Southerners wanted greater equity, but northerners feared that a trade war would most negatively impact their region's shipping industry.

The bills moved through both houses of Congress and were reconciled to the relative satisfaction of both sections. Madison was disappointed not to win discrimination against Great Britain, and would continue the fight during the entire decade. The revenue bills passed on July 4, with taxes on molasses, distilled spirits, and several other goods. Congress assessed a tonnage tax of six cents per ton on American vessels and fifty cents per ton on all foreign ships. The Tariff Act, largely the work of Hamilton, set import duties in the range of 5 to 10 percent with an additional tax on goods carried by foreign ships. Later that month, the Collection Act established the system of one hundred customs collectors to ensure the taxes were paid. The tariffs were aimed at protecting the shipping and manufactures of the nascent country and provided the vast majority of federal income for more than a century.

While Congress successfully navigated the sectional divide to produce a revenue during the celebration of American independence and nationhood, President Washington was recovering from an infection and swelling in his left thigh that was surgically removed and left him bedridden for weeks. He missed an event by the Society of Cincinnati at St. Paul's Chapel where Hamilton eulogized his friend, General Nathanael Greene, in an oration commemorating the anniversary of his death. Hamilton praised his friend and the glorious cause for liberty because the meritocracy of the Continental Army brought to light "talents and virtues which might otherwise have languished in obscurity or only shot forth a few scattered and wandering rays." That opportunity for greatness would become apparent as Hamilton rose to great heights in the Washington administration.

Washington was looking for a treasury secretary and first asked his close friend, Revolutionary financier Robert Morris, to accept the position. Morris, however, was deeply involved in wide-ranging investments around the globe. He advised Washington, "You will be no loser by my declining the secretaryship of the treasury, for I can recommend to you a far cleverer fellow than I am for your minister of finance in the person of your former aide-de-camp, Colonel Hamilton." Washington replied, "I always knew Colonel Hamilton to be a man of superior talents, but never supposed that he had any knowledge of finance." Morris responded: "He knows everything, sir. To a mind like his nothing comes amiss." Madison thought Hamilton "perhaps the best qualified for that species of business."

Washington informed Hamilton that he would be named the treasury secretary. Hamilton eagerly agreed, even though the salary of $3,500 would not equal his income as an attorney. But he was driven by a desire to serve the republic and put the public good above his private interest. He thought it "would be in his power in the financial department of the government to do the country great good and this consideration outweighed with him every consideration of a private nature." Hamilton would later write of his desire to win lasting fame as the founder who organized the finances of the new republic and laid the proper foundations of a prosperous economy. "I conceived myself to be under an obligation to lend my aid towards putting the machine in some regular motion. Hence I did not hesitate to accept the offer of President Washington to undertake the office of Secretary of the Treasury."

Hamilton understood the risks he was assuming when he accepted the position. "I hazard much, but I thought it an occasion that called upon me to hazard," he told Lafayette. The perils of a public life were evident to a person who had engaged the political controversies of the day for over a decade. Moreover, the hazards were not simply political disputes, but they jeopardized his reputation and fame if the experiment did not work. On the other hand, the potential lasting reward of historic reputation as a founder far outweighed the dangers.

On September 2, President Washington signed the bill authorizing the creation of the Treasury Department. On Friday, September 11, Washington officially nominated Hamilton as the nation's first secretary of the treasury, and the Senate confirmed him the same day. The new secretary dove into his responsibilities that weekend and arranged a fifty-thousand-dollar loan to the federal government from the Bank of New York, and requested another loan for the same amount from the Bank of Philadelphia. On September 21, the House of Representatives stated that "an adequate provision for the public credit" was a "matter of high importance to the national honor and prosperity." Therefore, the House asked Secretary Hamilton to prepare a report on the public credit for the next congressional session.

Hamilton was an administrative genius who had both a grand moral vision of his objectives related to building a prosperous economy and an eye for details and information that he would need to work toward achieving his vision. In his first few days in office, he worked feverishly on gathering information about the nation's economy, including customs collections from each state. He inquired into the collection of duties, the need for a Coast Guard to cut down on smuggling, and the amount of cargo in ship manifests. Five assistants, including Oliver Wolcott Jr. and William Duer, were quickly confirmed and helped him in these tasks enormously. Meanwhile, Hamilton had a staff of forty and some five hundred customs revenue collectors, inspectors, and supervisors, which made treasury by far the largest federal department.

Congress had achieved a great deal in setting up the new government during its first session. It had established the executive departments and confirmed President Washington's nominations. Besides the Treasury Department under Hamilton, Congress created the State

Department under Thomas Jefferson and the War Department under Henry Knox. Virginian Edmund Randolph became the attorney general. The Judiciary Act of 1789 created the federal court system, and Hamilton's friend, John Jay, became the nation's first chief justice of the Supreme Court. The Congress also passed the Bill of Rights to protect essential liberties and sent twelve amendments to the states for ratification. One significant debate that was left unresolved was the permanent location of the nation's capital, a symbol of unity and national Union. Most of the members advocated for their states or region. Hamilton wanted New York because it was the rising commercial center of the new nation.

George Washington was pleased by the accomplishments of the government that summer and by the relative unity that pervaded its councils. "It was indeed next to a miracle that there should have been so much unanimity, in points of such importance, among such a number of citizens, so widely scattered and so different in their habits in many respects, as the Americans were," he wrote to Catherine Macaulay Graham. "So far as we have gone with the new government (and it is completely organized and in operation) we have had greater reason than the most sanguine could expect to be satisfied with its success." Washington was rightly proud of the organization and achievements of the new government. On the other hand, whatever spirit of unity existed would soon be strained by the debate over the report on the public credit Hamilton was preparing at the behest of Congress. Washington toured the Northeast in late October, visiting several mills and early factories. He had a strong entrepreneurial bent and praised the growth of manufactures and commerce in a diverse economy that was essential to American prosperity. Hamilton had an advocate in the president for his financial vision. Hamilton would need all the help he could get in the coming struggle to establish the public credit.

CHAPTER 13

ESTABLISHING THE PUBLIC CREDIT

Hamilton launched into his usual prodigious effort in completing a major project. He studied the nation's failing credit from every angle and assembled a dizzying array of statistics. Correct information would allow him to develop the proper solutions and present a logical, airtight case. Hamilton also demonstrated the personal and professional honor and integrity that would characterize his tenure as treasury secretary. He knew at this early date that his political enemies would pounce on any appearance of impropriety. When Richard Henry Lee asked for insight into the report he was writing, Hamilton replied: "I am sure you are sincere when you say you would not subject me to an impropriety. Nor do I know that there would be any in my answering your queries. But you remember the saying with regard to Caesar's wife. I think the spirit of it applicable to every man concerned in the administration of the finances of a country. With respect to the conduct of such men—*suspicion* is ever eagle-eyed and the most innocent things are apt to be misinterpreted."

While Hamilton was applying himself scrupulously to the study of the nation's credit, he had conversations with a British diplomat that have been misinterpreted. Major George Beckwith traveled to the United States to warn of the termination of preferential treatment for U.S. shipping in British ports if Madison's retaliatory trade bills became law. Hamilton thought it was in the mutual interest of the

English-speaking nations to maintain strong ties whatever their recent experience. He believed that the United States was founded "upon principles, that in my opinion render it safe for any nation to enter into treaties with us, either commercial or political." That liberality extended to Great Britain in Hamilton's estimation, a belief that was not shared by many Americans such as Madison and Jefferson. The reasons for friendly relations with Great Britain were many. "I have always preferred a connection with you, to that of any other country," Hamilton intimated. "*We think in English*, and have a similarity of prejudices, and of predilections." Besides language ties and a shared culture, the Americans inherited the English tradition of liberty under law since Magna Carta.

While some historians believe that he conceded too much to Beckwith, Hamilton was tough and realistic in the conversations. He reminded Beckwith that Americans "are, and shall be, great consumers" of British goods, and thus the British had a strong interest in friendly commercial intercourse. Even though the United States was dependent on British trade and some 90 percent of its manufactured imports came from Great Britain, neither nation would benefit from a trade war. Hamilton warned against "a rigid adherence to your present plan to produce a system of warfare in commercial matters." He reminded Beckwith that, "We are a young and a growing empire, with much enterprise and vigor." He also hinted that British mercantilist policies would force Americans to seek a trading partner and political connections with France. Clearly, the British would not want their main enemy to form an alliance with the Americans. "Connected with you, by strong ties of commercial, perhaps of political, friendships, our naval exertions, in future wars, may in your scale be greatly important—and decisive."

Hamilton surveyed a number of issues with Beckwith related to the unresolved issues in the Treaty of 1783. The Americans still had not paid their debts to British creditors and had confiscated Tory property contrary to the peace treaty. The British continued to occupy western forts and had not compensated slaveowners for escaped slaves. Hamilton also raised the importance of the United States acquiring free navigation of the Mississippi River, though this concerned the Spanish. Hamilton admitted that he did not have any official credentials to meet with Beckwith but encouraged the two nations to enter into talks for a formal treaty.

While Washington knew nothing of these initial conversations, and Hamilton was to a certain degree impinging upon the sphere of the secretary of state, Jefferson was not even in the country and would not assume the responsibilities of his office until March of the following year. Rather than undermining American foreign policy, Hamilton was strongly defending American interests at a critical stage. Hamilton later informed President Washington and Secretary Jefferson of continuing conversations with Beckwith as they formulated American foreign policy. Hamilton's diplomacy was rooted in enlightened American self-interest and natural law principles of justice. He also realistically assessed American strength, and decided that commercial ties and neutrality would necessarily predominate American diplomacy for the immediate future. As diplomatic historian John Lamberton Harper has written, "Hamilton's approach was grounded in the realities of the situation, that of a rising but vulnerable country, still liable to have its career as a great power nipped in the bud."[1]

Many congressmen understood that the crisis in American finances demanded attention. Representative William Loughton Smith of South Carolina argued that the country must meet its obligations: "We are not in a situation to determine whether we will or will not have a public debt. We have it already. . . . It follows, of consequence, that we must pay. . . . The only question that can come before us is, the mode of doing it." Representative Theodore Sedgwick warned that further delay would "be mischievous and destructive of the general welfare." Hamilton agreed with this consensus. Great evils would result from the nation's crushing Revolutionary War debt that threatened to bankrupt the new nation. Establishing the public credit was the first pillar in Hamilton's financial vision for a modern economy. The soundness of the nation's finances was essential for American prosperity, political stability, and national strength if the lessons of the Confederation period were any guide for the national honor and future greatness. With these goals in mind, he had amassed an incredible amount of information that he used to produce his torrent of forty thousand words in his *Report on Public Credit*.

On January 8, 1790, George Washington climbed aboard his coach, followed by Hamilton and others in their carriages, and traveled to Federal Hall, where the president presented his first State of the Union Address to Congress. Washington adopted an enlightened and comprehensive view of American economic progress that was in harmony with Hamilton's vision and provided a presidential endorsement of the report that was to come. His specific recommendations included a uniform currency, uniform weights and measures, postroads, useful inventions for the development of agriculture, commerce, and manufactures, the promotion of science, and a national university.

Washington was particularly supportive of establishing the national credit, which he endorsed to the House of Representatives. The president recommended congressional action on Hamilton's forthcoming plan because of the importance of establishing the national honor, prosperity, and national character:

> I saw, with peculiar pleasure, at the close of the last session, the resolution entered into by you, expressive of your opinion that an adequate provision for the support of the public credit, is a matter of high importance to the national honor and prosperity. In this sentiment I entirely concur. And, to a perfect confidence in your best endeavors to devise such a provision as will be truly consistent with the end, I add an equal reliance on the cheerful co-operation of the other branch of the Legislature. It would be superfluous to specify inducements to a measure in which the character and permanent interests of the United States are so obviously and so deeply concerned, and which has received so explicit a sanction from your declaration.

A few days later, on January 14, the clerk of the House of Representatives read the *Report on Public Credit*. It probably killed Hamilton not to read it personally, laying out its principles and explicating each of its parts logically while deflecting the expected firestorm of criticism from those who were ignorant of the requisite financial expertise. The most important moral principle that animated the report was the national honor of the United States. The national debt was a sacred obligation that bound Americans by their honor to pay. The "good faith" of the United States and its "punctual performance of contracts" was essential to confidence in the new nation at home and abroad. Hamilton observed, "States, like individuals, who observe their engagements, are respected and trusted, while the reverse is the fate of those who pursue an opposite conduct." Indeed, the national credit was inextricably bound to the national honor by "the immutable principles of moral obligation" just as it was bound to personal honor. He believed that following the natural law would promote virtue and happiness. "In the order of Providence, an intimate connection between public virtue and public happiness, will be its repugnancy to a violation of those principles," he wrote. This upright and liberal policy would "promote the increasing respectability of the American name" and "answer the calls for justice."

Besides the core value of the national honor, the *Report on Public Credit* was grounded on additional objects. Hamilton argued that an adequate provision for the public debt and its proper extinguishment would achieve several goals. Generally, it would restore confidence and open channels of productive industry. Greater confidence in American credit would help to strengthen property values and the value of the currency. In addition, a sound national credit would allow the United States to enjoy lower interest rates and borrow on easier and cheaper terms, thereby freeing capital for productive investments. Agriculture and manufactures would thus grow, which, in turn, would benefit domestic and foreign commerce internally. These practical economic considerations would have larger political advantages for the United States. The public credit would "cement more closely the union of the states" and provide "security against foreign attack." Therefore, Americans would enjoy prosperity and political stability at home, and national security abroad.

Hamilton made an accounting of the national debt and came to the staggering amount of $79 million. The federal government owed $29 million in principal and $11.4 million in interest, the United States owed $12 million including $1.8 in interest to the French and Dutch for loans from the Revolutionary War, and the thirteen states owed about $25 million. Modern scholars have slightly revised the amount downward, but it was a close rendering of the total debt. For

Hamilton, the debt incurred by the federal government and states fighting the war was "the price of liberty" and the "faith of America has been repeatedly pledged for it, and with solemnities, that give peculiar force to the obligation."

The accounting of the debt was the easy part; the difficulty was finding just and equitable ways of retiring it. The debt owed to foreign countries from unpaid loans was relatively straightforward, and Hamilton believed a consensus existed to pay it "according to the precise terms of the contracts relating to it." The first significant controversy was that some states had paid their Revolutionary War debts and others had not. Another source of contention was that many veterans had been paid in Continental securities but had sold their certificates when wartime inflation caused their value to drop. Speculators had purchased the certificates for ten or twenty cents on the dollar and would gain handsomely from gambling on the "distresses" of the soldiers. Hamilton proposed means of reconciling all the debt and doing as much justice as circumstances would permit and larger goals dictated. He demonstrated great prudence in weighing the conflicting principles and interests involved.

Hamilton first engaged the arguments over "redemption" of the federal securities purchased by speculators from the soldiers who originally held them. He argued that paying the original holders of the debt would be "equally unjust and impolitic, as highly injurious" to the soldiers, the speculators, and the public. The soldiers had property rights in the certificates and had made free use of the property in the marketplace. "That the case of those, who parted with their securities from necessity, is a hard one, cannot be denied," Hamilton admitted. However, others may have had little faith in the Confederation government and sold them to invest in other opportunities. Regardless of their motivations (which could not now be determined), they were willing to sell the securities for present gain. It would be a practical nightmare to try to discover the original holders as the supporters of "discrimination" advocated. The speculators for their part had purchased the certificates in good faith, paying what they were worth in the market, and assumed the risk that the certificates would never be paid. Indeed, the speculators invested in a "revolution in government" creating a more perfect Union that paid its obligations.

Hamilton thought paying the original bondholders was "inconsistent with justice, because in the first place, it is a breach of contract." It would also be "repugnant to an express provision of the Constitution of the United States" that provision for all debts made under the former government be honored. He warned that violating the sanctity of contracts and violating the constitutional rule of law would be unjust and would have a "fatal influence" on the public credit.

The second controversy related to the Revolutionary War debt was his plan for the "assumption" of the state debt by the federal government. Hamilton addressed the issue that some states were still debtors and some were creditors by requiring payment from those states that owed money and crediting those who had already paid their wartime debt. Moreover, Hamilton argued that, "It appears difficult to conceive a good reason, why the expenses for the particular defense of a part in a common war, should not be a common charge, as well as those incurred professedly for the general defense. The defense of each part is that of the whole." If an accounting was made for differing monetary contributions to the war, a calculation also had to be made for states suffering worse damage than others. In short, the costs of war had to be equally shared by all. Hamilton also thought the policy of the federal government assuming the debt of the states as "a measure of sound policy and substantial justice" that would provide "an orderly, stable, and satisfactory arrangement of the national finances." The federal government would be the sole creditor and would collect the revenue to extinguish the debt, thereby strengthening the federal government and national Union.

After making his arguments for redemption and assumption of the debt, Hamilton then proposed means of paying off the debt. He posited that "the proper funding of the present debt, will render it a national blessing" because it would restore the public credit and promote the productive engines of the American economy. But public debts, like private ones, could invite "prodigality" and were "liable to dangerous abuse." Therefore, he thought it was "a fundamental maxim in the system of public credit of the United States, that the creation of debt should always be accompanied with the means of extinguishment."

Hamilton proposed paying the debt through various taxes as well as refinancing schemes. He expected substantial revenue from import duties that Congress passed the previous summer. In addition, he proposed a variety of consumption taxes on wine, spirits, tea, and coffee. New foreign loans at lower interest rates would refinance the foreign debt owed to other nations. Moreover, Hamilton recommended lowering the interest rates paid on federal bonds from 6 to 4 percent, which substantially reduced the amount of money the government would pay out in the coming years. Investors would accept the lower rate because they would benefit considerably from much greater confidence in the value and trustworthiness of their investments. They could also buy and sell the securities in the open market, creating the basis for the New York Stock Exchange. Business historian Thomas McCraw argues that Hamilton was taking a big gamble on the future of American prosperity, but gives Hamilton's plan high marks. Hamilton "understood better than any other founder—indeed, better than any other American of his generation who left enough records to judge—how everything in the national economy was related to everything else. A first-class student of both economics and administration, he saw that in the construction of grand strategy, every move must be coordinated so as to make the whole of public policy exceed the sum of its parts."[2]

The reactions to the plan in Congress and across the country were consistent with Hamilton's expectations. Nationalists and financiers praised the plan. Fisher Ames called it "a masterly performance" and appreciated its protection of property rights, the sanctity of contracts, and national honor. Robert Morris, who had struggled for years to make the independent nation financially stable, argued Hamilton did an admirable job. "Credit, public credit particularly, is a jewel so invaluable as to exceed all price," Morris wrote, and invested himself in securities that were to be redeemed.

Others were mortified by the proposed financial plan. Pennsylvanian Benjamin Rush wrote to Madison: "I sicken every time I contemplate the European vices that the Secretary's gambling report will necessarily introduce into our infant republic." Rush thought the infamy of the report would rank with the horrors of slavery or British tyranny. William Maclay predicted the "villainous business" would "damn the character of Hamilton as a minister forever." Richard Henry Lee thought Hamilton's "political tricks" would create a mountain of debt and vices "encouraged by wanton expeditions, wars, and useless expenses." Madison concurred with Lee, privately writing that a "public debt is a public curse, and in a representative government a greater than in any other."

The ire loosed against the report was particularly focused on redemption. Representative James Jackson of Georgia launched a vehement diatribe against the plan for what he saw as great injustice against America's veterans. "Look at the gallant veteran, who nobly led your martial bands in the hour of extreme danger," he beseeched Congress. "See him deprived of those limbs which he sacrificed in your service! And behold his virtuous and tender wife, sustaining him and his children in a wilderness, lonely, exposed to the arms of savages, where he and his family have been driven." The beneficiaries of the ungrateful, monstrous injustice were speculators who were "as rapacious as wolves." Jackson could barely contain himself. "My soul rises indignant at the avaricious and immoral turpitude which so vile a conduct displays." Jackson may have been one of the most emotional and outspoken of the critics of redemption, but he was not alone.

The heated debate continued throughout the rest of the month and into the next. On February 11, the more sober and moderate Madison rose in the House and offered a more rational critique of the plan offered by his former nationalist ally and coauthor of the *Federalist*. Madison started his speech asserting that public debts were an evil that must be removed as fast as possible. But Madison tried to have it both ways on discrimination. "The sufferings of the military part of the creditors can never be forgotten, while sympathy is an American virtue." He thought there was "something radically immoral" about not redeeming their value for the "gallant earners of them." On the other hand, Madison was a man of principle who believed in natural law and was forced to admit the government had a duty to pay the current holders of the debt. "No logic, no magic, could dissolve this obligation." He proposed a compromise on redemption—the present holders would receive the face value of the certificates while the soldiers would receive the difference between the face value and the present market price. "This will not do perfect justice," Madison conceded, "but it will do more real justice, and perform more of the public faith, than any other expedient proposed." Hamilton was dumbfounded by the opposition of his former collaborator, who was instrumental in creating a stronger national government. The debate was interrupted by the equally divisive issue of Quaker slave petitions, but the vote on Madison's compromise proposal for discrimination was held on February 22, and decisively defeated.

The debate over assumption began the next day and split the House of Representatives for months that spring. The issue stirred up the fierce debates between Federalists and Anti-Federalists over the increased power of the federal government and the sovereignty of the states. Opponents warned that power would be centralized in the national government at the expense of the states. Moreover, injustice would be done toward veterans and states that had extinguished their war debt. In late March, Jefferson arrived in New York and joined forces with Madison from within the administration. Hamilton's supporters despaired that the plan would fail. On April 12, the key vote on assumption lost by only two votes, 31-29. Stunned representatives who supported the plan reportedly had tears in their eyes and despondent looks on their faces.

Congressional opponents painted an image of greedy speculators who were sweeping the land, buying up bonds from gullible sellers, in the hope of making a killing. One complained that the spirit of speculation had "invaded all ranks of people." Members of Congress were not immune to purchasing the debt, raising questions of corruption and conflict of interest. Hamilton thought it odd that there were criticisms of Americans investing in the future of the new nation. "It is a strange perversion of ideas . . . that men should be deemed corrupt and criminal for becoming proprietors in the funds of their country. Yet I believe the members of Congress very small who have ever been considerably proprietors in the funds."

The deadlock continued through June, and assumption lost several more votes. It seemed a dead issue. The debate over the permanent location of the national capital was also bogged down, setting the stage for a possible bargain.

Thomas Jefferson related the events, as he remembered them, of the famous June 20 dinner party that led to the Compromise of 1790. He supposedly met Hamilton who had a "somber, haggard, and dejected" look. The two spoke of the failure of the assumption plan, and Hamilton tried to convince Jefferson of its "indispensable necessity towards a preservation of the union." Hamilton proposed to make common cause on the funding plan because "the administration and its success was a common concern." Jefferson explained that he considered the problem and tried to bring Madison and Hamilton together for a civil conversation on the matter. He invited them to dine with him that evening, and the antagonists agreed. Over excellent food and wines, Jefferson opened the conversation about the argument over assumption. Jefferson remembered that they found common ground for a compromise. Madison would vote against assumption but offered his general acquiescence to the bill. Since the trio recognized that the "pill would be a bitter one to the Southern states," they agreed to locate the permanent capital on the Potomac. Jefferson related that Madison persuaded a few of the southern opponents to relent on assumption, while Hamilton spoke with Robert Morris to help convince the Pennsylvanian delegation to concede a capital along the Potomac. Jefferson promised, "This is the real history of the assumption."

Many historians have their doubts about whether Jefferson's story is accurate and even whether the dinner party took place. Other historians note that other meetings were just as important as the famous dinner. Tench Coxe, Hamilton's assistant in the Treasury Department, met with Madison and Jefferson in early June to assuage their objections to assumption. Moreover, in mid-June, Virginia and Pennsylvania delegates met and negotiated the deal that made Philadelphia the temporary capital for ten years in exchange for a permanent capital on the Potomac. As Joseph Ellis notes in his Pulitzer Prize–winning book, *Founding Brothers*, "The [meetings] we do know about demonstrate conclusively that the compromise reached over Jefferson's dinner table was really the final chapter in an ongoing negotiation that came together because the ground had already been prepared."[3] Historians Stanley Elkins and Eric McKitrick agree: "The evidence prompts the conclusion that all things considered there is really no better shorthand for what happened than the story told by Thomas Jefferson."[4]

As a result of the Compromise of 1790, the residence bill won approval on July 10. Hamilton won his assumption bill when it passed the Senate a few days later and narrowly passed the House on July 26. Hamilton was disappointed that New York would not be the nation's capital, but he was elated that he had won the first part of his planned financial system. He understood how close he had come to failure. "Had a single session [of Congress] passed . . . without some adequate provision for the debt the most injurious consequences were to have been expected." For his part, Jefferson later bitterly regretted the compromise and disingenuously told Washington: "I was duped into it by the Secretary of the Treasury and made a tool for forwarding his schemes, not then sufficiently understood by me, and of all the errors of my political life this has occasioned me the deepest regret."

CHAPTER 14

THE NATIONAL BANK

Secretary Hamilton had little time to rest on his laurels for the hard-fought victories of redemption and assumption. In the late summer and early autumn of 1790, he was busy packing up the Treasury office and moving to the temporary capital in Philadelphia. The new office was on Third Street between Chestnut and Walnut, and he moved into a nearby home in October. In August, the Congress requested the treasury secretary to prepare another financial report. Hamilton and his staff spent the next several months producing another massive report, this one proposing to create a national bank.

When Hamilton was composing his report, the United States had only a few banks—in Philadelphia, Boston, and New York. The country suffered from a bewildering array of state, national, and foreign currencies including Spanish doubloons, Dutch guilders, British pounds, and French guineas. Counterfeiting was rampant, and the unscrupulous "clipped" coins to steal a portion of their precious metal content. More importantly, specie was in short supply, and agriculture, business, and commerce consequently suffered a dearth of available credit and loans for productive investments.

Hamilton's *Report on a National Bank* was submitted to Congress on December 14, and was another masterful blueprint for American prosperity and energetic government to stimulate the private markets and common good. Hamilton believed it was sound public policy rooted in free enterprise and republican principles. The national bank was modeled after the Bank of England and other "enlightened commercial nations," though it was a uniquely American creation. Hamilton spent time countering anticipated objections to the proposed bank, but he did not engage the question of constitutional legitimacy in any significant manner. Instead, he focused on the pragmatic policy grounds of the bank.

The most important function of the national bank would be "the augmentation of the active or productive capital of a country." Hamilton explained the basic workings of a bank. Individuals would profitably invest money in the bank, which, in turn, would lend out part of that money to borrowers taking out loans to invest in (hopefully) productive enterprises. The new economic activities would, in turn, create more investment opportunities. Hamilton argued that, "By contributing to enlarge the mass of industrious and commercial enterprise, banks become nurseries of national wealth."

The benefit of the increased economic activity would be to increase the circulation of money in the economy. Hamilton was an advocate of issuing paper currency based upon the reserves of gold and silver in the bank. Citizens would thus have a medium of exchange that would facilitate daily trade that would benefit the economy generally.

The republican government, and thus the American people, would also benefit from having a national bank. It would gain the critical advantage of funding during times of "dangerous and distressing emergencies." Hamilton obliquely referred to the American experience during the Revolutionary War and the great stresses of runaway inflation, unpaid armies, and inadequate specie caused by the lack of a national bank until some benefits were gained under the Philadelphia Bank of North America in 1781. The "public safety and welfare" demanded a national bank in times of war. Moreover, Hamilton asserted that the bank would help facilitate the collection of taxes.

After arguing the principles and utility of the Bank of the United States, Hamilton then explained its framework. The national bank would receive an exclusive charter as a limited-liability corporation for twenty years, after which representatives in Congress could decide whether to recharter the bank. It would be capitalized at $10 million, which was several times the capital of the existing banks combined. Government deposits would comprise $2 million, and private investors would purchase the other $8 million in stock. Investors could purchase one-quarter of the shares with gold and silver, and the other three-quarters with government bonds paying 6 percent interest. The bank would facilitate the payment and collection of federal taxes and import duties, loan money to the United States, and serve as the government's sole depository. It would accept deposits and lend out the money based upon fractional reserves. It would issue notes that served as currency based upon its gold and silver reserves. It would have branches in several cities to loan money throughout the country in different enterprises. A twenty-five-member board would be private individuals not public appointees. Moreover, it would operate for the private profit of investors. Hamilton thought, "It appears to be as essential ingredient in its structure, that it shall be under a *private* not a *public* direction, under the guidance of *individual interest*, not of *public policy* . . . liable to being too much influenced by *public necessity*." This would avoid the temptation of the government to print money in emergencies and cause inflation as happened during the Revolutionary War. Therefore, the bank, not the treasury, would issue currency.

The bank needed tax revenues to service the interest payments on the bonds. He proposed increased duties on imported and domestic spirits. Country stills would be taxed, though there was an exemption for home consumption. Fortunately, Hamilton had the support of Madison on the revenue issue. Madison guided the excise tax on distilled spirits through the Congress in the spring of 1791.

Many southerners opposed the creation of the bank, believing that it would only benefit northern speculators. Across the nation, opponents of the Hamiltonian financial plans warned that the bank would be an engine of a corrupt moneyed aristocracy that would ruin the American republican character. One member of Congress predicted, "This bank will raise in this country a moneyed interest at the devotion of government; it may bribe both states and individuals." James Jackson of Georgia argued the bank was "calculated to benefit a small part of the United States, the mercantile interest." Senator William Maclay predicted it would become "an aristocratic engine" and a "machine for the mischievous purposes of bad ministers." The Whig vision of corrupt banks and government ministers plotting against the liberties of the people still resonated in the 1790s.

Hamilton had advocates who supported his continental vision of an energetic national government helping to lay the foundation for a prosperous economy. Fisher Ames said, "It seems to be conceded within doors and without that a public bank would be useful to trade, that it is almost essential to revenue, and that it is little short of indispensably necessary in times of public emergency." He also argued for implied powers in the Constitution. "Not exercising the powers we have, may be as pernicious as usurping those we have not." He did not "pretend that it gives any new powers; but it establishes the doctrine of implied powers." He thought "that construction may be maintained to be a safe one which promotes the good of the society, and the ends for which the government was adopted, without impairing the rights of any man, or the powers of any state."

The debate was fierce but short in the Senate. The Federalist-controlled Senate easily passed the bank bill on January 20. The bill was liable to encounter hostility from southerners in the House. James Madison again led the charge against the bank in Congress and against Hamilton's financial and constitutional vision in general.

On January 28, Hamilton proposed a less controversial *Report on the Mint* to Congress. The recommendations for establishing a national mint met little opposition because America suffered a bewildering array of foreign and state coinage and needed a uniform currency. The report combined Hamilton's usual deep research and administrative knowledge and expertise. The variety of coins he suggested would allow all Americans to participate in the market economy. Hamilton also wanted the national coinage to give Americans a greater sense of nationhood with its symbols prominently displayed.

On February 2, Madison delivered a lengthy speech in the House questioning the constitutionality of the proposed bank. He worried that it imitated what he considered the corrupt British system of banking. He also stated that Congress did not have the constitutional authority to establish a bank because it was not an enumerated power of Congress in Article I, Section 8. The Constitution was "a grant of particular powers only, leaving the general mass in other hands," he said. Even though he admitted that the clause was limited to means that were "*incident* to the *nature* of the specified powers," he rejected the argument that the powers of the bank were related to congressional enumerated powers of laying and collecting taxes, paying debts, or borrowing money on the credit of the United States. The Necessary and Proper Clause did not apply in Madison's view. "The latitude of interpretation required by the bill is condemned by the rule furnished by the Constitution itself." He thought "at most it could be but convenient," but was not necessary or proper. The proposed bank would destroy "the essential characteristic of the government, as composed of limited and enumerated powers."

In making this argument, Madison reversed his position in the 1780s for a stronger national government and his specific argument in the *Federalist* for implied powers. He wrote in *Federalist #44*, "Had the convention attempted a positive enumeration of the powers necessary and proper for carrying their other powers into effect; the attempt would have involved a complete digest of laws on every subject to which the Constitution relates; accommodated too not only to the existing state of things, but to all the possible changes which futurity may produce; For in every new application of a general power, the particular powers, which are the means of attaining the object of the general power, must necessarily vary with that object." He continued with a succinct assertion of what he called the axiomatic truth of implied powers: "No axiom is more clearly established in law, or in reason, than that wherever the end is required, the means are authorized; wherever a general power to do a thing is given, every particular power necessary for doing it, is included."

Madison made other speeches against the bank bill but to no avail. On February 8, the House of Representatives passed the bill by an overwhelming vote of thirty-nine to twenty generally along sectional lines. The controversial bill seemed to be on its way to becoming a law when it was questioned by a somewhat unlikely person in President Washington.

President Washington was a firm advocate of a stronger national government and wholly shared Hamilton's political and financial vision and policies. However, Washington was scrupulous about following the Constitution and laying down precedents according to a constitutional rule of law. The arguments Madison made in Congress and opposition by Secretary of State Jefferson and Attorney General Edmund Randolph questioning the constitutionality of the bill troubled Washington. The absence of a specific clause enumerating the power to establish a bank made him proceed cautiously. He even asked his friend and ally in Congress, Madison, to draw up a veto message in case he decided to exercise that power. He judiciously took the concerns seriously and solicited the opinions of Hamilton and the opponents in the cabinet to help him render a decision about signing the bill. The president had not yet vetoed a bill and would not exercise this power lightly.

Since Washington only had ten days to decide whether to sign the law, the cabinet members rapidly produced their opinions and submitted them to the president. Randolph offered two rambling papers in which he argued that the bank was unconstitutional because it was not an enumerated power of Congress, the Necessary and Proper Clause did not support it, and the Tenth Amendment limited the federal government to enumerated powers. Jefferson's ideas mirrored those of his friend, Madison. The secretary of state, invited to comment on a field outside of his area of responsibility, cited the Tenth Amendment. He argued that to "take a single step beyond the boundaries thus specially drawn around the powers of Congress, is to take possession of a boundless field of power, no longer susceptible of any definition." The power to establish a bank was not one of the delegated powers of Congress, nor did the Necessary and Proper Clause apply because he thought the powers of the bank were unrelated to any other powers in Article I, Section 8. Jefferson argued that it was neither strictly necessary nor proper: "A bank therefore is not *necessary*, and consequently not authorized by this phrase." He advised Washington to veto the bill as an "invasion of the legislature." The strict-constructionist argument posed by Jefferson was his attempt to restrict the powers of the national government narrowly and resist Hamilton's centralizing policies.

On February 16, after weighing the papers submitted by Jefferson and Randolph, Washington forwarded them to Hamilton and invited the treasury secretary to consider them while composing his defense of the bank bill's constitutionality. The result was another *tour de force* and demonstrated Hamilton's full talent to write brilliantly crafted state papers about constitutional and economic issues. After a weekend of extraordinary effort, on Monday, February 21, he informed the president he had been "sedulously engaged" cranking out his "thorough examination" over the previous few days and delivered a final copy by Wednesday.

The *Opinion on the Constitutionality of a National Bank* was rooted upon the Hamiltonian view of energetic government with both expressly enumerated powers and related implied powers for the national government to exercise the means to achieve its ends of such powers. Hamilton argued that Jefferson's reading of the Necessary and Proper Clause was so restrictive that, "There are few measures of any government, which would stand so severe a test." On the other hand, Hamilton read the clause according to what he called a "sound maxim of government" that the constitutional powers of the national government "which concern the general administration of the affairs of a country, its finances, trade, defense, etc., ought to be construed liberally, in advancement of the public good." However, he argued that his loose construction was not a recipe for unlimited government or tyranny. "For no government has a right to do *merely what it pleases*." He detailed several clauses of Article I, Section 8 to show how they were related to the powers of the national bank and met the constitutional standard of the congressional power "To make all laws which shall be necessary and proper for carrying into execution the foregoing powers." Since the power for the national government to establish a bank was supported by Article I, Section 8, in his view, Hamilton thus argued it was part of the sovereign and supreme powers of the national government in the Supremacy Clause of Article VI. The Jeffersonian vision, he argued, would "furnish the singular spectacle of a *political society* without *sovereignty*, or of a people *governed* without *government*." Instead, Hamilton wanted the "*means* requisite . . . to the essential ends of political society."

Washington had only a few days to read Hamilton's lengthy opinion and compare it with the judgments rendered by the other cabinet officers. After deliberating on the divergent views, Washington agreed with Hamilton's constitutional judgment. Washington and Hamilton had shared the belief that the national government had been too weak to achieve its objects and the public good during the Revolutionary War and Confederation periods. They sought to empower a more energetic, though constitutionally limited, government that would advance the public good and vigorously provide for the common defense, a prosperous economy, and a stable republican political order.

As scholar Carson Holloway writes: "On Hamilton's view, the Constitution was intended to remedy the embarrassments and incapacity of the federal government under the Articles of Confederation. Energetic government requires not merely a Constitution with adequate powers but also an adequate exercise of those powers." On Friday, February 25, President Washington signed the bank bill into law.

"At issue for both men," Holloway writes, "was not only the bank itself but the very nature of American constitutionalism and the possibility of good government."[1] This divide between Hamilton and Jefferson over the Constitution, the purposes of government, and national economic policies became the basis for the growing ideological divisions that resulted in the first political parties.

In late June, Hamilton had sanguine expectations for subscriptions to the bank stock. "In all appearances, the subscriptions to the Bank of the United States will proceed with astonishing rapidity. 'Twill not be surprising if a week completes them." The bank stock was offered on the market on July 4, and investors bought up all the shares immediately.

The Jeffersonians were disgusted by the spectacle of what they deemed speculators growing rich from a corrupt government institution. They viewed the entire episode through the lens of radical Whig ideology from the American Revolution. In early August, Madison wrote to Jefferson: "The stock-jobbers will become the praetorian head of the government, at once its tool and its tyrant, bribed by its largesses and overawing it by clamors and combinations." Jefferson agreed with his friend's assessment and denounced the "spirit of gaming."

The fears of the Jeffersonians appeared to be justified in August when the bubble burst and the stock market collapsed. Hamilton bought up some shares to restore confidence in the market, but the public trust was damaged when it came to light that his assistant, William Duer, engaged in insider trading and gobbled up shares to enrich his friends. It was the last thing that the secretary of treasury needed, considering the controversy surrounding the bank. Hamilton prided himself on strictly upright and honorable acts at his department and rebuked Duer. "I will honestly own I had serious fears for you—for your *purse* and your *reputation* and with an anxiety for both I wrote to you in earnest terms."

Hamilton plunged into writing the last of his major financial reports in Washington's first term and delivered the *Report on Manufactures* in December. Congress had directed him to "prepare a proper plan . . . for the encouragement and promotion of such manufactories as will tend to render the United States independent of other nations for essential, particularly for military, supplies." The report was the grandest example of Hamilton's comprehensive financial vision for the United States. Hamilton envisioned a diversified national economy for the entire Union. The centerpiece of the report was developing American industry, but Hamilton wanted to tie together the agricultural, commercial, and industrial parts of the economy into a united whole. Moreover, the plan would provide high wages in productive outlets for workers in different areas of the economy, including women, children, and immigrants. The government would play a vital role in bringing this vision to reality—by protecting innovation, protecting American manufactures from foreign competition, and spending money on internal improvements such as roads and canals to facilitate trade and link markets. The result would be an integrated, prosperous modern economy that would greatly enhance American military strength, and promote national independence and honor. The growing United States would be an economic and military powerhouse in world affairs and ready to protect its national sovereignty and rights.

Hamilton had a powerful patron for his ideas in President Washington. As historian Edward Lengl has pointed out, Washington was an entrepreneur who wanted to believe that, "Americans' native talents would come to the fore in building an industrious 'Land of freedom.' The government's role was to establish the conditions conducive to prosperity."[2] In his First Annual Message back in January, Washington had supported domestic manufacturing and industry. Like his treasury secretary, he advised government measures for the "advancement of agriculture, commerce, and manufacturing" to achieve a diversified but unified economy. He spoke of importing "new and useful inventions from abroad, as to the exertions of skill and genius in producing them at home; and of facilitating the intercourse between the distant parts of our country." The safety of a free people and national security required "such manufactories, as to tend to render them independent on others, for essential, particularly for military supplies." In other words, the president wanted the government to build a powerful, integrated, and independent fiscal-military state capable of confronting the European nations.

But Hamilton had his opponents too. They expressed great fear that the assumption of state debts, the creation of a national bank, and now the promotion of manufacturing and internal improvements were leading to a dangerous centralization of power in the federal government. Not surprising, Jefferson and Madison took the lead against Hamilton's proposal by questioning the constitutional basis for his plan. "If not only the means, but the objects are unlimited," Madison complained, "The parchment had better be thrown into the fire at once." In his discussions with the president, Jefferson began openly questioning Hamilton's centralizing policies and wondering if they were a plot for unlimited government or monarchy. Many others agreed with these concerns, and the controversial report failed to gain any traction in Congress and died. However, the Hamiltonian vision of government promotion of manufactures, protective tariffs, and internal improvements was later taken up by Whigs in the nineteenth century. It was no less contested by Jefferson's political heirs in the Democratic Party.

That summer Hamilton had worked with his assistant treasury secretary launching the Society for Establishing Useful Manufactures. At the heart of this experiment was the creation of a model industrial town along the Passaic River and Falls in Paterson, New Jersey. The incorporated community sold stock to investors and received a state charter for a monopoly and tax breaks. The capital would be invested in mills and early factories to use machinery to produce a wide variety of textiles including rugs, blankets, and stockings. Skilled artisans would be drawn to work and reside in the company town. Hamilton hoped that it would be emulated throughout the country, but it failed due to the corrupt mismanagement of William Duer and a financial panic the following year.

Whatever his upright public integrity, that summer, Hamilton fell prey to some dishonorable temptations. Twenty-three-year-old Maria Reynolds appeared unannounced at his Philadelphia home and asked to speak with Hamilton in private. They went into a separate room where Maria spun a tale of being an abused and abandoned wife. Her husband, James Reynolds, had taken all her money so she had none to travel with to live with some friends in New York. Acting chivalrously, Hamilton believed her story and brought some money to her home that evening. Hamilton was shown upstairs to her bedroom, and, as he later put it, "some conversation ensued from which it was quickly apparent that other than pecuniary consolation would be acceptable."

Hamilton and Reynolds began an adulterous affair that lasted several months. He rendezvoused with her frequently that summer at her house and at his home once Eliza and their four children had fled to the Schuyler mansion in upstate New York to escape the heat of Philadelphia. Reynolds told Hamilton that she was reconciling with her husband and that he had engaged in shady dealings with insider information while at treasury. Hamilton struggled mightily with the affair, knowing that it was wrong, but was driven by violent passions and distressed at the thought of it ending. Maria Reynolds played on Hamilton's conflicting emotions "with a most imposing art." He finally discovered that she had used her wiles to seduce Hamilton and make him the "dupe of a plot" for blackmail.

James Reynolds pretended to have discovered the affair and wrote Hamilton: "I am very sorry to find out that I have been so cruelly treated by a person that I took to be my best friend instead of that my greatest enemy. You have deprived me of everything that's near and dear to me." He finished, "Now I am determined to have satisfaction." The Reynolds couple threatened to tell Eliza and began demanding blackmail payments. Hamilton was willing to pay because he could not stand the thought of hurting his wife with revelations of the affair. "No man tender of the happiness of an excellent wife could, without extreme pain, look forward to the affliction which she might endure from the disclosure, especially a public disclosure, of the fact." However, he dissuaded her from returning home several times that summer so that he could continue the liaison. He admitted, "The truth was that . . . I dreaded extremely a disclosure—and was willing to make large sacrifices to avoid it."

Hamilton was also concerned about the possible damage to his public reputation and the destruction of the financial edifice he worked so hard to build. After meeting with Reynolds and being told that one thousand dollars would satisfy the cuckolded husband's "wounded honor," Hamilton felt he had no other choice and scraped together the payment in December and January. Hamilton made additional payments until the following June. When Reynolds and Jacob Clingman, a former clerk of Speaker of the House Frederick Muhlenberg, were jailed some months later for defrauding the Treasury Department, the affair came to light.

Speaker Muhlenberg, Senator James Monroe, and Representative Abraham Venable confronted Hamilton at his office to discover if he was involved in misconduct with the jailed pair. Hamilton stridently denied any wrongdoing in his public capacity and offered to meet at his home with them that evening. There he painfully admitted the scandalous extramarital affair and extortion payments to silence Reynolds. He insisted on detailing the entire affair to exonerate himself and remove the slightest doubt that he had engaged in any violation of the public trust. The three congressmen were apparently satisfied by Hamilton's account. Monroe explained, "We left him under an impression our suspicions were removed. He acknowledged our conduct toward him had been fair and liberal—he could not complain of it." Hamilton accepted their word that the matter would remain confidential and thought that the affair was over.

CHAPTER 15

AMERICA DIVIDED

While Hamilton struggled with his personal scandal, he was subject to an increasingly hostile organized political reaction against his policies, his vision for America, and his political philosophy. Thomas Jefferson led the charge against Hamilton and orchestrated a behind-the-scenes campaign to destroy him personally and politically. Jefferson was frustrated that Hamilton had much greater influence with the president in formulating policy and that Washington and Hamilton shared a common vision for the country. Hamilton defended his public policies to create the American republic on proper foundations and his personal honor against the assaults. Hamilton's view of the future with an energetic, constitutional central government, diversified and dynamic economy, and amity with Great Britain rather than revolutionary France contrasted sharply with Jefferson's vision of independent small farmers, state sovereignty, and an antipathy toward the British in favor of the French revolutionaries. This set the two at odds and helped to create the first political parties.

Ironically, the founders had a universal antipathy toward political parties, which were equated with "factions." The founders believed that parties were engines of individual self-interest rather than patriotic devotion to the public good. Parties stirred passions and division rather than reason and harmony. Even though the founders all attacked parties, the Democratic-Republicans led by Jefferson and the

Federalists led by Hamilton emerged only a few years into the early republic. The Revolutionary consensus about liberty and self-government gave way to fierce partisan divisions over the formulation of domestic and foreign policies in the 1790s. The members of both parties believed that they were purely interested in the public good while the other side was the illegitimate "party" or "faction" interested only in their own power and interest. In this poisonous atmosphere, both sides questioned each other's motives and policies, and engaged in political intolerance unwilling to understand the other side or compromise. Each side demonized the other and questioned their patriotism. After all, they believed that the survival of the American republic was at stake and endangered by their political enemies.

Jefferson was genuinely alarmed by the success of Hamilton's assumption and redemption plans, the proposals for federal support of manufacturing and internal improvements, and his general sympathies for the British. He believed that Hamilton and his allies were conspiring to introduce a monarchy and aristocracy in the United States that would destroy American liberties. Jefferson started organizing a quiet campaign to oppose Hamilton's centralizing policies. In the spring of 1791, Jefferson and Madison toured New England supposedly on a botany tour but really to meet with several politicians who were sympathetic to the antifederal point of view and the coalescing opposition to the administration. In addition, Jefferson hired Philip Freneau, supposedly as a translator in the State Department. In truth, he was employed to serve as the editor of a partisan newspaper to attack administration policies. The *National Gazette* started publishing in the fall of 1791, and Jefferson saw it as a counter to the "Toryism" of John Fenno's proadministration *Gazette of the United States.*

In early 1792, Jefferson began complaining directly to President Washington and warning him of a monarchist plot surrounding the administrative policies of Alexander Hamilton. In late February, Jefferson warned Washington that Hamilton was acquiring "such an influence as to swallow up the whole executive powers" from within the Treasury Department. Hamilton's financial plans were corrupting the American republican government, introducing "a species of gambling, destructive of morality, and which had introduced its poison into the government itself." Jefferson asked whether "we live under a limited or unlimited government."

Washington was an upright constitutionalist and trusted his advisors to carry out policies for the good of the republic. He knew each of them for decades and thought all of them working hard to set the right precedents in their respective departments. Still, he was concerned by Jefferson's charges against Hamilton and took them seriously, even though he had doubts about the accusations. Washington was also weary of being president and wanted to retire. The signs of disunity in his administration were deeply troubling, especially since it forced him to consider serving another term as a unifying force in a divided government.

In May, Jefferson pestered Washington with even stronger allegations that Hamilton was a monarchist seeking to overthrow the republic. The ultimate object of Hamilton's "corrupt squadrons" was to "prepare the way for a change from the present republican form of government, to that of a monarchy, of which the English constitution is to be the model." Even now, they were using the monstrous federal debt as a "means of corrupting both branches of the legislature." Washington was tiring of such accusations and retorted that he took the criticisms personally because he had signed many of the bills into law. He was insulted by the implication that he was a dupe of Hamilton in the major measures of his administration.

Hamilton caught wind of the partisan attacks and grew progressively defensive. "Mr. Madison cooperating with Mr. Jefferson is at the head of a faction decidedly hostile to me and my administration, and actuated by views in my judgment subversive of the principles of good government and dangerous to the union, peace and happiness of the country," he explained. For several decades in war and peace, Hamilton avowed, he was "affectionately attached to the republican theory" as a lawgiver and was deeply wounded that his patriotic motives were being questioned.

In turn, Hamilton questioned Jefferson and Madison's views as "equal[ly] unsound and dangerous." He particularly thought their foreign policy views threatened the national security of the United States. "They have a womanish attachment to France and a womanish resentment against Great Britain . . . and they would risk the peace of the country in their endeavors to keep us at the greatest possible distance from the latter." Characteristically, Hamilton also wrote several anonymous newspaper articles defending his policies and attacking those of his political enemies.

In the middle of the summer, Washington enumerated the Jeffersonian grievances for Hamilton and invited him to respond to Jefferson. The president wanted reassurance that they were pursuing right policies. Hamilton's answers affirmed administration policies, yet Washington was still disturbed by the squabbling and divisions that tore at his cabinet. He pleaded with both men for greater moderation and generosity in their opinions of each so that his administration would enjoy greater harmony. He hoped "there might be mutual forbearances and temporizing yieldings on all sides." It was his "earnest wish" that "balsam may be poured into all the wounds which have been given to prevent them from gangrening."

Hamilton and Jefferson both denied that they were responsible for the feud and blamed the other for launching the attacks disrupting political harmony. Jefferson upped the ante, making vicious personal attacks on Hamilton, questioning his patriotism. "I will not suffer my retirement to be clouded by the slanders of a man whose history, from the moment at which history can stoop to notice him, is a tissue of machinations against the liberty of the country which has not only received him and given him bread, but heaped its honors on his head." Hamilton fired back in the pages of the *Gazette of the United States* that Jefferson was an "intriguing incendiary" and "aspiring, turbulent competitor" who was quietly an ambitious Caesar.

Washington was depressed that neither man would yield for the good of the administration. The president badly wanted peace but still seemed to side with Hamilton. Jefferson's unending assertions that Hamilton was at the center of a monarchist plot struck the president as particularly unhinged. On October 1, Jefferson had breakfast at Mount Vernon and leveled the tiresome charges at his political opponent. Washington snapped back that he "did not believe there were ten men in the United States whose opinions were worth attention who entertained such a thought."

For Washington, the meeting was proof that Jefferson would not relent in thinking Hamilton a barely closeted monarchist plotting to overthrow the government. For Jefferson, it was additional proof that Washington was so thoroughly deceived by Hamilton that he could not see plain evidence of Hamilton's wrongdoing. By this time, Washington agreed to serve a second term because of the crises facing the country and the bitter partisan divisions within the government.

Washington shared with Madison his intent to retire and asked him to write a "valedictory address." Madison at first pled against retirement but agreed finally to draft the address. Hamilton joined the many voices urging Washington to remain in office. Hamilton bluntly appealed to the president's patriotism to serve the republic: "I trust, Sir, and I pray God that you will determine to make a further sacrifice of your tranquility and happiness to the public good." On December 5, Washington was again chosen unanimously to be president contrary to his wish to retire after his first term. John Adams defeated Hamilton's old political nemesis, George Clinton, for the vice presidency. Hamilton watched the election carefully, and while no fan of Adams, favored the vice president over Clinton, who was "a man of narrow and perverse politics" and "opposed to national principles."

During the winter of 1792, Hamilton was finalizing his *Report on Manufactures* to Congress and trying to persuade the members to pass the program for an integrated national economy. Moreover, he was in the dangerous grip of an adulterous affair involving extortion. The national election consumed his attention as well. Finally, he had a growing family.

If Hamilton had any time to reflect on his achievements during the first administration, he would have good reason to be proud. The branches of the national government were governing the country effectively, and the economy was booming. He had not traveled an easy path over the past four years with significant opposition to his financial plans and a few economic hiccups along the way. But he had worked closely with President Washington to craft administration policies that successfully achieved peace and prosperity.

Hamilton had good reason to be pleased that his patron Washington had agreed to serve a second term and could count on strong influence in shaping administration policy. This also meant that his political enemies were alert to his political power and ruthlessly pursued his destruction. Tensions over the French Revolution in Europe were also heating up and threatened to drag the United States into war. Domestically, political divisions were splitting the country along ideological and sectional lines. The economic policies of the Washington administration were also stimulating opposition on the frontier and imperiled law and order. During the second term, Hamilton would continue to work closely with the president to face a host of challenges.

CHAPTER 16

THE GENET AFFAIR

Hamilton did not have to wait long before he was embroiled in several controversies as the new year dawned. His *Report on Manufactures* was dead on arrival. It contemplated too large a role for the federal government for a Congress that was growing skeptical of his centralizing economic policies. His political enemies were organizing against him and questioning his public integrity, and therefore his honor. It was an inauspicious start to the new administration.

Thomas Jefferson and James Madison enlisted the aid of Virginia representative William Branch Giles to launch an investigation of Treasury in the House. The House questioned Hamilton's use of foreign loans to repay a government loan from the national bank. The treasury secretary answered and explained his actions to its satisfaction. Then, in late January, Giles introduced five resolutions demanding a complete accounting of the government's dealings with the bank within a few weeks. Hamilton felt his honor and integrity challenged.

Giles thought that Hamilton could not comply so quickly. Giles imagined that the public accusations and appearance of impropriety would at least destroy Hamilton's public reputation and discredit him in the court of public opinion. The congressman greatly underestimated his opponent. Hamilton worked at his feverish pace to draw up the massive reports with an airtight accounting of the transactions that showed not an iota of any financial malfeasance. Jefferson and Giles did not relent in their offensive and drew up nine resolutions of censure against the treasury secretary for gross maladministration in office. Meanwhile, Jefferson lobbied Washington to demand an official investigation and was rebuffed. Members of Congress recognized that the resolutions were a transparent partisan smear job. On March 1, Hamilton was vindicated when a pathetic five congressmen, including Giles and Madison, voted for the censure resolutions. Hamilton proved himself an upright and honest public servant. Jefferson persisted in his attacks on Hamilton and would not rest until he thwarted what he perceived as Hamilton's monarchist designs.

In the coming months, a foreign policy crisis would consume the attention of Washington and his cabinet. A world war caused by the French Revolution and the execution of Louis XVI threatened to drag in the United States because of American trade with Europe and the 1778 treaties with France. The foreign policy crisis confronted the Washington administration and forced it to formulate an appropriate American response and foreign policy principles for America's role in the world. A mission by Minister "Citizen" Edmond Charles Genet forced the administration's hand because of his arrogant diplomatic style. The Genet "affair" further enflamed the passions of a divided and highly partisan country. The contentious debate over supporting Great Britain or France in the war split the administration.

Many Federalists initially praised the French Revolution, though they noted its bloody character from its inception. Hamilton was mixed in his view of events in France. "I have seen with a mixture of pleasure and apprehension the progress of the events which have lately taken place in your country," he confided to Lafayette. Hamilton celebrated the revolution as a "friend to mankind and liberty," but he also had a "foreboding of ill." As a profound thinker about human nature and politics, Hamilton was disconcerted by the ties of the radical French Enlightenment to the violence of the revolution tearing down the old regime. "I dread the reveries of your philosophic politicians who appear in the moment to have great influence and who being mere speculat[ors] may aim at more refinement than suits either with human nature or the composition of your nation." His dread of the murderous character of the revolution was confirmed by the September Massacres, the storming of Tuileries, and regicide. In the spring of 1793, he lamented, "Would to heaven that we could discern in the mirror of French affairs, the same humanity, the same decorum, the same gravity, the same order, the same dignity, the same solemnity, which distinguished the course of the American Revolution."

On the other hand, Jefferson was swept away by the ideals of the French Enlightenment and early stages of the revolution when he was in France, and enthusiastically welcomed the violent overthrow of the regime. He continuously excused the bloodshed and excesses in the name of progress for the rights of man. In one unhinged letter completely divorced from reality in early 1793, Jefferson even asserted: "The liberty of the whole earth was depending on the issue of the contest, and was ever such a prize won with as little innocent blood? My own affections have been deeply wounded by some of the martyrs to this cause, but rather than it should have failed I would have seen half the earth desolated. Were there but an Adam & Eve left in every country, & left free, it would be better than as it now is." Even with revelations of organized state violence by the guillotine during the Terror, he hoped that the triumph of the revolution would "bring at length kings, nobles and priests to the scaffolds which they have been so long deluging with human blood." With such starkly differing views of the French Revolution, the two most dominant members of Washington's cabinet were bound to clash over American foreign policy.

In 1793, the United States was weak militarily and ill-prepared for war. Hamilton recognized this and advised President Washington to adopt a course of neutrality. Despite his reputation for being partial to Great Britain and for warmongering, Hamilton instead spent the better part of the decade arguing for neutrality in American foreign policy by means of peace through strength. He preferred a course in which the United States continued its internal national development as a young republic and benefited from expanding its international trade as a neutral. While Presidents Washington and John Adams implemented this path, the European powers largely rejected it, and the belligerents attempted to disrupt American trade with their respective enemies without much regard for American neutral rights. As the eminent diplomatic historian George Herring wrote: "Washington and his successor, John Adams, set important precedents in the management of foreign and national security policy. Conciliatory at the brink of war, they managed to avert hostilities with and wring important concessions from both England and France. . . . The Federalists' conduct of U.S. foreign policy significantly shaped the new nation's institutions and political culture. Through skillful diplomacy and great good fortune, the United States emerged from a tumultuous decade much stronger than at the start."[1]

The new French republic dispatched Genet to the United States with instructions meant to draw the United States into the war on its side as a sister republic. Genet was to remind the United States of its 1778 treaty obligations and demand the Americans immediately pay three million dollars of its outstanding debt. Genet was also to outfit privateers in American ports and haul prizes there. He was even to commission Americans to join in driving the British and Spanish soldiers out of Canada, Louisiana, and Florida to liberate them. This mirrored the armies of France presently attempting to liberate the people of Europe from monarchy. Genet expected great American enthusiasm for his mission and French ambitions, but was told to influence public opinion if necessary. The provocative instructions were bound to clash with the Washington administration's desire to remain neutral; Genet's haughtiness would ensure a diplomatic row.

Genet sailed into Charleston harbor aboard the *Embuscade* on April 8 to a great popular frenzy of support. South Carolina governor William Moultrie welcomed the French minister, allowing him to commission four privateers with unmistakably pro-French names—*Republican, Anti-George, Sans-Culotte,* and *Citizen Genet*—to capture British prizes and haul them back to Charleston. For the next ten days, the prominent officials of the city entertained the minister. Genet's belief that he had unqualified American support was greatly fortified. He was not soon disabused of this notion. He departed for Philadelphia by carriage and was wildly received by swollen crowds along the way.

That same day, Washington met with his cabinet to discuss the appropriate American stance on Genet, the treaties with France, and the European war. Washington had been inaugurated for his second term and then departed for Mount Vernon. Before he left, he instructed Jefferson to receive Genet "without too much warmth or cordiality." The president wrote Hamilton and Jefferson soliciting their opinions on declaring neutrality and the status of the French treaties. While Jefferson neglected to respond, Hamilton quickly replied and dominated the course of the discussion by drawing up thirteen questions that Washington brought to the cabinet meeting.

The cabinet was of course split on several important questions but came to an agreeable consensus. Hamilton argued that the 1778 treaties were made with the monarchy and were invalid after France changed its political regime. He wanted to avert war and argued strenuously for a proclamation of neutrality since the nation was ill-prepared for war and could trade with both sides. Predictably, Jefferson took the opposite view and maintained that the treaties with the valuable ally were still in effect. He thought the administration should receive Genet and opposed neutrality. Washington listened carefully to his advisors. He agreed with Jefferson that the treaties were valid and that the administration would receive the French minister without qualifications. On the other hand, he would issue a proclamation of neutrality, with a small concession to Jefferson that he would not use the word.

President Washington issued the proclamation of neutrality a few days later, signaling that the United States would not favor one side or the other but would claim the rights of neutrals. "The duty and interest of the United States require, that they should with sincerity and good faith adopt and pursue a conduct friendly and impartial toward the belligerent powers." He warned American citizens not to take action that would contravene the spirit of the message. Swept up by Genet and partisan passions, the Democratic-Republicans disregarded the message. Madison called the proclamation a "most unfortunate error." Jefferson thought that Congress had the exclusive power over war and peace, and argued only Congress could issue such a proclamation. Hamilton and Washington knew that the president had great constitutional latitude over the conduct of American foreign affairs. The greater challenge, however, was preserving the nation's neutrality in face of violations by both belligerents. For now, they had their hands full with a French minister whipping up enthusiasm for war on American soil.

The French immediately challenged neutrality. The *Embuscade* towed two British prizes into Philadelphia only days later, causing Jefferson to gloat that "thousands and thousands of the yeomanry of the city crowded and covered the wharves . . . they burst into peals of exultation." Meanwhile, two French privateers were equipped in Charleston with American crewmen. Washington scrambled to call a cabinet meeting to consider the provocations. The episode fueled the internal debate between Hamilton and Jefferson. The secretary of state defended the French right to capture British vessels in American waters, while Hamilton argued that such a course would compromise American neutrality and be a cause for war. The frustrated president split the difference, allowing the French to keep their prizes but deny U.S. ports to future ones.

On May 16, Genet finally arrived in Philadelphia. The following day, a "vast concourse" of citizens welcomed him into the city and were not disappointed to hear his passionate appeal to the rights of man and the common cause of liberty. On May 18, Washington officially received Genet coolly in contrast with the wild popular frenzy. Genet felt that he lived "in the midst of perpetual fetes" as Republican citizens held large dinners for the minister replete with the singing of the Marseillaise, the firing of cannon, and countless toasts to the French Revolution. The heady adulation he received only convinced Genet that he could expect the Americans to comply with his every wish. Jefferson gushed, "It is impossible for anything to be more affectionate, more magnanimous than the purport of his mission." He said Genet "offers everything and asks nothing."

Hamilton was disgusted by the display and thought the crowd was smaller than announced. Moreover, the crowd was filled with rabble-rousers. "With very few exceptions, they were the same men who have been uniformly the enemies and the disturbers of the government of the United States." With some overblown rhetoric in the overheated atmosphere, he suspected that the zeal for France was "intended by every art of misrepresentation and deception to be made the instrument of controlling, finally of overturning the government of the Union."

Jefferson regretted encouraging Genet to press the United States on supporting France. Although the secretary of state tried to help Genet navigate American politics, the arrogant minister indignantly protested any measure that did not give him carte blanche to win support for the war against Great Britain. The pair exchanged increasingly heated letters in early June, which left Jefferson exasperated. He informed Genet

that French privateers would have to leave American waters and that
the United States would not make any advance payments on its debt.
Genet indignantly counseled against "the cowardly abandonment of
their friends in the moment when danger menaces them, but in adhering strictly, if they can do no better, to the obligations they have contracted with them." Genet promised to respect Washington's opinions
but only until "the representatives of the sovereign people shall have
confirmed or rejected them." When Jefferson responded with a lengthy
missive about the rights of neutrals and explained the administration
would not allow armed ships to depart American ports with prizes,
Genet delivered an explosive rebuttal. Hamilton called it "the most
offensive paper, perhaps, that ever was offered by a foreign minister to
a friendly power, with which he resided."

Still, the outrages continued. Genet outfitted an expedition of
Americans against the Spanish in the West. He also outfitted and
armed a captured British prize, *Little Sarah*, in the port of Philadelphia
and rechristened it as the privateer *Petite Democrate*, contrary to the
president's orders. Jefferson wrote somewhat disingenuously to James
Monroe that, "I am doing everything in my power to moderate the
impetuosity of his movements, and to destroy the dangerous opinions
which has been excited in him, that the people of the United States will
disavow the acts of their government, and that he has an appeal from
the Executive to Congress, and from both to the people." Jefferson
waffled between prodding Genet and wincing at his actions because he
was systematically undermining the French cause in America.

The Pennsylvanian authorities, and Hamilton, Jefferson, and
Knox all sought to warn Genet not to let the *Petite Democrate* sail. The
minister flew off the handle, promising to put to sea and threatening
to go over the head of the president directly to the American people.
Washington was returning from Mount Vernon, and his cabinet was
characteristically split on how to react. Hamilton and Knox wanted
to set up a battery that would blast the ship out of the water if it tried
to sail away, while Jefferson tried to conciliate the explosive situation.
Hamilton thought that it was "pernicious and disgraceful" to be made
into an "instrument of the hostilities of France" against Great Britain.

An irate Washington arrived in Philadelphia and called a cabinet
meeting. He exclaimed, "Is the Minister of the French Republic to

set the acts of this government at defiance, with impunity and then threaten the executive with an appeal to the people?" Washington feared irreparable damage to American national honor. "What must the world think of such conduct, and of the government of the United States in submitting to it?" At this point, the administration settled for vigorously asserting American neutral rights and informing the French government of its minister's offensives.

Washington was also maddened by the partisan attacks on the administration in Republican newspapers. Washington told Jefferson "that by God he had rather be in his grave than in the present situation," and that, "he had rather be on his farm than to be made emperor of the world, and yet that they were charging him with wanting to be a king. That that rascal Freneau sent him three of his papers every day, as if he thought he would become the distributor of his papers, that he could see in this nothing but an impudent design to insult him."

Hamilton composed a series of essays under the pseudonym Pacificus to refute the partisan attacks on the administration as well as defend American neutrality. He argued that the president had a great deal of constitutional latitude to conduct the country's foreign policy and defended presidential authority to issue a proclamation of neutrality. "The duty of the executive to preserve peace till war is declared; and in fulfilling that duty, it must necessarily possess a right of judging what is the nature of the obligations which the treaties of the country impose on the government; and when in pursuance of this right it has concluded that there is nothing in them inconsistent with a state of neutrality, it becomes both its province and its duty to enforce the laws incident to that state of the nation." He also argued the United States was too weak and ill-prepared to go to war. "Self-preservation is the first duty of a nation," he wrote.

Jefferson hysterically cried, "Nobody answers him and his doctrine will therefore be taken for confessed." He begged Madison to respond: "For god's sake, my dear sir, take up your pen, select the most striking heresies, and cut him to pieces in the face of the public. There is nobody else who can and will enter the lists with him."

Madison belatedly responded with the *Helvidius* essays after the furor over Genet had died down. He thought the task of writing these essays was "the most grating one I ever experienced." In the essays,

Madison opined that Washington had exceeded his constitutional executive powers over war and peace that rightfully belonged to Congress. But, it was not his best performance. Even Madison said that it had been "of no advantage either to the subject or to the author," and that Hamilton had won the debate.

Jefferson admitted to Madison that Genet was a disaster for steering the administration toward a pro-French foreign policy. "Never in my opinion, was so calamitous an appointment made . . . hot headed, all imagination, no judgment, passionate, disrespectful, and even indecent towards the president in his written as well as verbal communication, talking of appeals from him to Congress, from them to the people, urging the most unreasonable and groundless propositions, and in the most dictatorial style, etc., etc., etc."

On August 1, the cabinet agreed that Genet must be recalled. Even Jefferson admitted "the necessity of quitting a wreck which could not but sink all who should cling to it." He privately noted that the minister's behavior was "indefensible by the most furious Jacobin." Jefferson was perhaps most deeply concerned about the consequences of Genet's scandalous mission on the Republican Party and finally abandoned him. However, Hamilton learned that the Terror had the guillotine awaiting Genet upon his return and magnanimously suggested to Washington to grant the minister asylum. Jefferson decided to retire after this exhausting series of events. At the end of September, Jefferson informed the president of his intention to resign but agreed to remain in office a few more months through the end of the year.

Genet's mission served to help the Washington administration define the principles of American foreign policy. While Jefferson won a few specific points along the way during the formulation of policy, Hamilton's vision of neutrality in European affairs and desire to avoid being too closely aligned with the violent French Revolution accorded perfectly with Washington's own views. The crisis helped to cement the common foreign policy principles between Washington and Hamilton and confirm Hamilton's influence on the president instead of Jefferson. Indeed, the crisis drove the main dissenting view out of the administration and unified it even more.

That summer, a yellow fever epidemic swept through the capital. Hamilton and Eliza contracted the disease while their children were sent away to the Schuyler mansion. Jefferson took a partisan swipe at his political enemy, stating, "A man as timid as he is on the water, as timid on horseback, as timid in sickness, would be a phenomenon if his courage, of which he has the reputation in military occasions, were genuine. His friends, who have not seen him, suspect it is only an autumnal fever he has." That was rich stuff coming from the man who fled Monticello in the face of approaching British troops during the Revolutionary War.

In 1793, the foreign policy crisis had consumed much of Hamilton's attention. The administration had resolved the Genet Affair satisfactorily by avoiding war and preserving the national honor. However, a domestic insurrection would challenge the administration and internal peace during the coming year.

CHAPTER 17

SUPPRESSING THE WHISKEY REBELLION

Domestic crises also plagued Washington's second administration that challenged the constitutional rule of law and further escalated partisan feelings. In the late spring of 1794, farmers in the western counties of Pennsylvania on the frontier angrily combined to resist the 1791 excise taxes on whiskey. Hamilton believed the taxes had been necessary for revenue to discharge the assumed national debt and that tariffs could not be raised any higher without discouraging trade. The representative Congress had passed the taxes on a bipartisan basis through majority rule. The taxes were clearly constitutional under congressional powers in Article I, Section 8. The president had signed the taxes into law.

The farmers on the frontier had a different view of the taxes. The mostly Scots-Irish settlers were fiercely independent and resented taxes passed by a distant central government. Most led a hardscrabble life and distilled their grain into whiskey because they had difficulty getting their perishable crops to eastern markets, especially since the Spanish controlled the Mississippi. Whiskey was used as a medium of exchange, and the yeoman farmers bitterly opposed a tax on the stills in their small operations. They had a disproportionate number of stills in the country and felt they unequally bore the brunt of the odious tax. As historian Thomas Slaughter points out, they deeply abided by revolutionary principles of liberty and self-determination.

They distrusted authority, and were prepared as their revolutionary fathers to resist the taxes.[1]

Washington issued a 1792 proclamation denouncing the violent proceedings on the frontier that were obstructing "the operation of the laws of the United States for raising a revenue upon spirits . . . enacted pursuant to express authority delegated in the Constitution of the United States, which proceedings are subversive of good order, contrary to the duty that every citizen owes to his country and to the laws, and of a nature dangerous to the very being of a government." The president had been horrified by Shays' Rebellion and decided that this new threat to the rule of law in the new republic must be curbed before it undermined the government. He called on his fellow citizens to "refrain and desist from all unlawful combinations and proceedings whatsoever having for object or tending to obstruct the operation of the laws." Washington saw it as his constitutional duty as chief executive to enforce the laws of Congress. Like many others, Washington also was anxious that the British, Spanish, and French were each plotting to separate the West from the eastern states to dismember the nascent United States and facilitate the collapse of the national Union.

Hamilton was especially concerned that the rebellion was strongest "in the state in which is the immediate seat of government." He agreed with the president that it was "absolutely necessary that laws, and the of the government to put them into execution." Hamilton was not only concerned about American precedents, but he was particularly worried about any popular violence while tens of thousands were murdered during the Reign of Terror in France. He unapologetically stood for law and order in a chaotic time. It was understandable that he wanted to enforce the rule of law and prosecute violators vigorously. His personal honor and the integrity of his financial plan were also at stake as the author of the excise taxes. He had even tried lowering the excise rates, but still the farmers were not pacified by anything but repeal.

In the summer of 1794, a wave of frontier violence erupted in western Pennsylvania. On July 15, federal marshal David Lenox and excise collector General John Neville were preparing to serve writs on several individuals to appear in Philadelphia for nonpayment of taxes. At daybreak the following morning, a mob of fifty armed men descended on Neville's home. Much like the revolutionary mobs in Boston, they demanded Neville's resignation and tax records, which they intended to destroy. When Neville refused, gunfire erupted. One person in the crowd was killed, and several were wounded in the shootout.

More than five hundred enraged locals wielding rifles and clubs surrounded the home the following day. A dozen soldiers from Fort Pitt defended the home, and another deadly gunfight resulted in more casualties on both sides. After the frightened guards surrendered, the crowd torched the mansion and surrounding buildings as Neville fled for his life. Lenox was kidnapped for a while until the farmers coerced him into not serving any papers and leaving the region with Neville. These were only the most outrageous terrorizing acts. Others included closing the federal courts, tarring and feathering, setting up mock guillotines, and threatening to march on the federal arsenal in Pittsburgh. In the wake of the violence, radical meetings were held, issuing fiery warnings against all federal authority in the area. On August 1, an estimated seven thousand farmers gathered at Braddock's Field. No one knew what they were prepared to do.

Word of escalating violence in western Pennsylvania trickled back to Philadelphia and frightened the administration. On August 2, Washington was sufficiently alarmed to call the cabinet into session. Hamilton quickly responded to a presidential request for an appropriate response with a written memorandum suggesting nationalizing the militia and sending an army of twelve thousand to suppress the rebellion (because the regular army was engaged fighting Native Americans further west). "It appears to me that the very existence of government demands this course and that a duty of the highest nature urges the chief magistrate to pursue it."

While preparing to send a force out west, Washington moderately dispatched a three-man commission headed by the attorney general to negotiate with the rebels. In addition, the president issued a proclamation calling out the militia of several states to counter the "overt acts of levying war against the United States," but calling on the rebels to cool their passions and "disperse and retire peaceably to their respective abodes." He favored a statesmanlike appeal to their good sense while energetically using the powers of his office to threaten a show of force to compel obedience to the law.

Hamilton also picked up his pen and wrote his customary essays to shape public opinion. Writing under the pseudonym of "Tully," Hamilton reiterated the argument that the federal government must defend the constitutional order and rule of law. The violent resistance of the insurgents, he warned, would leave the federal government prostrate and the laws trampled. The most sacred duty of citizens and the surest security for liberty, he argued, was an "inviolable respect for the Constitution and laws." Anarchy and factionalism by a violent minority would usher in a despotic government of force and endanger liberty. "There is no road to *despotism* more sure or more to be dreaded than that which begins at *anarchy*," he warned. Publius had made the same argument in the *Federalist* that a weak government and anarchy were often a greater threat to liberty than energetic government.

Washington patiently dispatched a peace commission, but its failure led him to request the governors of four states to mobilize their militias for an army to march west to quell the insurgents. That army of more than twelve thousand troops assembled in Carlisle in September. Hamilton organized preparations because he was temporarily heading the War Department when Secretary of War Henry Knox was on leave. The commander-in-chief rode as far as Carlisle to meet the army and then returned to Philadelphia. Hamilton remained with the army throughout the march, though General Henry Lee commanded.

Hamilton wrote to his sister-in-law from an encampment that he was on his way "to attack and subdue the wicked insurgents of the west." He sincerely believed that attempting to subvert the rule of law in the constitutional republic was an evil act. He correctly noted that the "large army has cooled the courage of those madmen." Trying to impress the lovely Angelica, he boasted, "In popular governments 'tis useful that those who propose measures should partake in whatever dangers they may involve. 'Twas very important there should be no mistake in the management of the affair—and I might contribute to prevent one." His personal honor and the national honor were at stake, and asserted by manly action.

The rebels dispersed in the face of this overwhelming show of force, and the army arrested only twenty rebels. Of these, two were convicted of treason. Washington generously granted clemency for the two ringleaders and pardoned them, since he had proven the national government capable of quelling the domestic insurrection and enforcing the law.

The scattering of the rebels back to their homes without a shot being fired tempted several leading Democratic-Republicans to advance the belief that the Federalist-dominated administration, and their favorite whipping boy, had overreacted. Employing the republican fear that standing armies were a threat to liberty, James Madison complained that the insurrection was used to "establish the principle that a standing army was necessary for enforcing the laws." Jefferson expressed the idea that the Federalists were chasing phantoms to strengthen federal power and stated, "An insurrection was announced and proclaimed and armed against, but could never be found." The same could be said of his later presidential crusade against Aaron Burr for treason in the West. Later historians have largely adopted the opposition view of the Whiskey Rebellion. For example, in their book on Washington's presidency, James MacGregor Burns and Susan Dunn posit that "the Whiskey Rebellion was never a true rebellion: it was oratory, mass meetings, and whiskey itself that largely kept the rebels going." They argue that the administration's actions represented a "spectacular military overreaction."[2]

Hamilton and Washington took a contrary view and believed there was a real threat brewing that needed to be curbed by decisive action to preserve republican government. Washington was defending majority rule and a consensual government of Congress. The president warned that if "a minority (a small one, too) is to dictate to the majority there is an end put, at one stroke, to republican government." Like Hamilton, Washington used the language of personal honor in his duties of leadership as president: "Neither the military nor civil government shall be trampled upon with impunity whilst I have the honor to be at the head of them." The president also understood that European governments were hoping for the collapse of the American republic and actively working toward this goal. Protecting the constitutional rule of law in the United States sent a message to the world that "republicanism is not the phantom of a deluded imagination: on the contrary, that under no form of government, will laws be better supported, liberty and property better secured, or happiness more effectually dispensed to mankind."

Washington was not above partisanship in seeing both the insurrection as a product of Democratic-Republican criticism of the administration's policy. In his annual message to Congress in November, the president blamed the rebellion as the "first formidable fruit of the Democratic societies" that had been highly active in the Genet Affair and were strong on the frontier during the Whiskey Rebellion. The passions, suspicions, and jealousies the societies aroused were antithetical to the public good and could "shake the government to its foundations."

CHAPTER 18

RETIREMENTS

I n December, Hamilton was in a reflective mood with domestic peace restored and anticipating his own retirement from the treasury. He was pleased that the rebellion had been "most happily terminated" without bloodshed. "The insurrection will do us a great deal of good and add to the solidity of everything in this country." Contrary to the contemporary and historical view that statements like this proved Hamilton continually manipulated crises like the Whiskey Rebellion to centralize federal power, good government at home and an enduring republic in world affairs required the right precedents of energetic government and stability for national strength.

As the treasury secretary and Washington's right-hand man over the past five years, Hamilton had pause to consider the state of the union from a long-range perspective and proudly assess his own role in the political and economic prosperity of the country. "All is well with the public. Government has gained by it reputation and strength, and our finances are in a most flourishing condition. Having contributed to place those of the nation on a good footing, I go to take a little care of my own; which need my care not a little."

He had labored and served the republic to establish it on solid foundations under constant scrutiny and relentless attack by his political enemies but had succeeded brilliantly in shaping the policies of the new constitutional government. But, as with many founders, public service had caused his own personal finances to suffer, and he needed to pay greater attention to them for his growing family. Moreover, Eliza had a difficult pregnancy and a miscarriage while he was with the army on the frontier, and he wanted to tend to his wife. Finally, he had endured years of wearying personal and political attacks questioning his Americanism, calling him a monarchist, and castigating his honesty and integrity as treasury secretary. Hamilton devoted himself to his law practice but would never dissociate himself from public affairs. He was too much of a political animal and longed to preserve the institutions he had painstakingly crafted over several years of Constitution-making and policymaking. His friend James McHenry offered some counsel to seek comfort and happiness. "What remains for you having ensured fame but to ensure felicity. Seek for it in the moderate pursuit of your profession."

Washington was no tool of Hamilton, but the president had depended on his brilliance for twenty years since the Revolutionary War. The president was sorry to lose his closest advisor and offered him sweeping praise for his public service. "In every relation which you have borne to me, I have found that my confidence in your talents, exertions, and integrity has been well placed. I the more render this testimony of my approbation, because I speak from opportunities of information which cannot deceive me and which furnish satisfactory proof of your title of public regard. My most earnest wishes for your happiness will attend you in retirement." He closed with the touching words, "You may assure yourself of the sincere esteem, regard, and friendship of, dear sir, your affectionate, George Washington."

Hamilton was touched by the expressions of confidence in his ability and honored to have lasting fame as a lawgiver, but he was embroiled in political controversy only months after his so-called retirement from public life. The United States faced new challenges to its neutral rights as Great Britain and France continued to struggle for European supremacy. The British tried to shut down American trade with the French enemy in the desperate world war. Unresolved tensions from the American Revolution and 1783 peace treaty contributed to the Anglo-American dispute. American planters still owed money to British merchants, while the British still had troops on the American frontier and had not compensated owners for runaway slaves during the war. Moreover, the Americans bristled at the feeling of colonial dependence due to persistent trade restrictions with the British Empire, especially the lucrative West Indian trade.

Throughout the diplomatic crises of the 1790s, Hamilton maintained a consistent stance on foreign policy. The primary consideration in his mind was to protect and advance American neutrality since the nation was still woefully unprepared for war and had to build its institutions. Amicable relations with the British were also a priority because he thought healthy commercial relations with the British were essential to American prosperity. Hamilton may have been an Anglophile, but he scrupulously defended American interests against any encroachments by the British or French. He was prepared to have the United States go to war, but peace offered the best course for the American republic. He would informally advise Washington on a course that supported American independence and sovereignty in a principled yet prudential and practical way.

The Jeffersonians pursued their own consistently anti-British policy. During the previous year, Madison had introduced resolutions in Congress for commercial reciprocity with all nations including Great Britain. If those agreements were not forthcoming from the British, as the Republicans expected, then the United States would slap retaliatory tariffs on them. The Republicans believed that the threat of a trade embargo would compel the British to open their empire to American trade. Since an embargo would probably hurt the Americans more than the British, it was a quixotic hope.

Hamilton worked behind the scenes to defeat Madison's resolutions, but his efforts were hampered by news that the British forbade neutral trade with the French and would intercept neutral vessels in the West Indies. The Royal Navy and privateers seized hundreds of American ships and impressed their sailors into service. Consequently, Hamilton advised Washington to raise a twenty-thousand-man army and temporarily suspend British trade because of the provocation. Still, he wanted to "preserve peace at all costs, consistent with the national honor." He did not want to go to war but defended an honorable peace based upon national strength. "To be in a condition to defend ourselves, and annoy any who may attack us will be the best method of securing our peace." Congress passed a thirty-day embargo on all shipping, and war seemed imminent. Scholar John Lamberton

Harper praises Hamilton's stance: "Hamilton was better able to appeal to Washington's instincts and to prevent the ship of state from sailing into a disastrous confrontation. . . . With a handful of others, he perceived that a seemingly hopeless situation was ripe for a diplomatic breakthrough. The spring of 1794 may have been his finest hour."[1]

The administration weathered this crisis with Hamilton advising Washington to avert war at all costs. The Republicans portrayed Hamilton as eager for war, but he warned that the Republicans were the war hawks animated by a spirt of revenge upon Great Britain. He soberly told the president that the United States was not prepared for war, and that the consequences were simply too unpredictable and potentially destructive for the new nation. "This country ought not to set itself afloat upon an ocean so fluctuating, so dangerous, and so uncertain but in a case of absolute necessity."

Washington concurred and pursued diplomatic solutions to the crisis. The British hardly wanted a war with the United States during the desperate world war with France and revoked the orders. Britain and her former colonies were open to resolving the present crisis and their unresolved issues peacefully. Washington prepared to dispatch a special envoy to Great Britain to negotiate and eventually selected Supreme Court Chief Justice John Jay. The president briefly considered Hamilton as his most trusted advisor but admitted Hamilton was a polarizing figure and "did not possess the general confidence of the country." When the Republicans protested Jay's appointment, suspecting a pro-British plot, Washington gave them a sop by sending James Monroe to France to replace Gouverneur Morris.

Hamilton's overriding goal was to defend American rights and national sovereignty. Proving again that he was not a tool of the British, he met with George Hammond and heatedly conveyed to the British minister that Americans would not indefinitely suffer British depredations to their trade, demanded indemnification for ship seizures, and vindicated neutral rights. Hamilton also helped to craft Jay's diplomatic instructions with other Federalists. The focus was again on a spirited defense of American rights and right to indemnification while resolving persistently to facilitate a commercial relationship. Scholar Karl-Friedrich Walling notes Hamilton's "sense of the national interest made him anxious to preserve peace with England more than any other country. . . . Until the United States was no longer dependent on England, peace with that country simply was a fundamental national interest, if not the most important foreign policy objective of the 1790s."[2]

The controversial Jay Treaty arrived in Philadelphia on March 7, 1795. Hamilton was fairly disappointed with the terms. The British agreed to evacuate the Northwest forts, submit claims for indemnification for escaped slaves and pre-Revolutionary War debts to international arbitration, and grant commercial concessions by opening the West Indies to ships smaller than seventy tons. The British refused to concede American neutral rights and stop their depredations against American shipping. The United States was simply in a weak bargaining position and had no navy to force the issue. Most historians today generally have a favorable view of the treaty because it bought the United States peace and was the best that could be secured under the circumstances. The reaction at the time, however, was decidedly negative.

Hamilton was primarily frustrated that the Jay Treaty did not wring stronger trade concessions especially in the West Indies in Article XII. Washington instinctively knew the Republicans would unleash a firestorm of opposition at the treaty and decided to keep its consideration by the Senate secret. He hesitated sending it to the Senate but eventually did so (without recommendation) because he thought it was the best that could be obtained. The Senate convened in a special session in early June, and after weeks of heated debate, ratified the treaty twenty votes to ten, narrowly meeting the constitutional mandate of a two-thirds vote. The body excised the insulting article limiting American trade in the West Indies to small vessels.

On July 1, Benjamin Franklin Bache's Republican newspaper, the *Aurora*, obtained a copy of the treaty and published its text to great public outrage. Madison said the reaction was "like an electric velocity" through "every part of the Union." Patriotic celebrations on the Fourth of July included the widespread burning of the treaty and of Jay in effigy, leading him to joke that he could walk the length of the eastern seaboard by the firelight. Washington wrote, "At present the cry against the treaty is like that against a mad dog." Republicans Madison and Jefferson predictably disparaged the treaty. Madison said it was "unworthy [of] the voluntary acceptance of an independent people." Jefferson detected monarchist sympathies and criticized the treaty as a "treaty of alliance between England and the Anglomen of this country against the legislature and people of the United States."

Washington sought Hamilton's views on the treaty and urged him to write essays defending it publicly against widespread criticism. Hamilton explained to Washington that, "With peace, the force of circumstances will enable us to make our way sufficiently fast in trade. War at this time would give a serious wound to our growth and prosperity. . . . It follows that the objects contained in the permanent articles are of real and great value to us."

In mid-July, Hamilton learned firsthand that the popular animus could turn violent when he tried to stump for the treaty. On July 17, he met with leading mercantile interests at a coffeehouse and planned a counterdemonstration to a gathering of treaty opponents the next day at City Hall. On the following afternoon, Hamilton courageously addressed a hostile crowd of an estimated five thousand New Yorkers. The crowd jeered him and hurled a volley of stones at him, one of which struck him in the forehead. He was ushered from the scene and retired in fear. As he was fleeing, he stumbled across a partisan disagreement in the street between a Federalist and Republican James Nicholson, father-in-law of Albert Gallatin. Hamilton foolishly joined the fray. A quarrel ensued with Nicholson denouncing Hamilton as "an abettor of Tories" and accusing him of cowardly ducking a duel. The hot-headed Hamilton eagerly accepted the challenge and intemperately joined another partisan fight. He quickly escalated tensions by threatening to fight each of the Republicans one by one. It was not Hamilton's proudest day.

In August, Washington unenthusiastically signed the treaty, but the partisan contest over the treaty endured. Hamilton's temper cooled from his street fights as he picked up his pen under the pseudonym "Camillus." He wrote at his usual torrid pace, publishing twenty-eight essays in the coming months. Washington praised the essays and thought Hamilton defended the treaty in "a clear, distinct, and satisfactory manner." Hamilton consistently articulated the principles of an honorable peace that advanced American commercial interests and avoided a destructive war because of his realistic understanding of American global power. "A very powerful state may frequently hazard a high and haughty tone with good policy, but a weak state can scarcely ever do it without imprudence. The last is yet our character, though we are the embryo of a great empire."

Jefferson was deeply concerned that Hamilton was winning the war for public opinion and urged Madison to respond. "Hamilton is really a colossus to the anti-republican party—without numbers, he is a host within himself. They have got themselves in a defile, where they might be finished; but too much security on the Republican part, will give time to his talents and indefatigableness to extricate them. We have only middling performances to oppose to him. In truth, when he comes forward, there is nobody but yourself who can meet him." Madison remembered the debacle of the Pacificus-Helvidius debate in which Hamilton had bested him on the debate over the neutrality proclamation and demurred.

Still, the Republicans bitterly attempted to railroad the treaty by using the rearguard action of the appropriation power in the House of Representatives to deny funding for the treaty. In early 1796, the Republicans in the House also demanded all the papers related to the treaty negotiations. Hamilton advised the president to fight the House on both measures. He argued that the proper constitutional treaty-making powers rested with the president, with the advice and consent of the Senate, not the House. Moreover, Hamilton counseled Washington to exert "executive privilege" and not submit the papers to the House. Doing so would set a precedent that would "be fatal to the negotiating power of the government, if it is to be a matter of course for a call of either house of Congress to bring forth all the communications, however confidential." Washington agreed, and claimed executive privilege. In April, the House voted for the appropriations without seeing the papers.

In May, Washington sent Hamilton a draft of a Farewell Address signaling the president's intention to retire from office. Madison had written the draft in 1792 when Washington had wanted to leave office, but circumstances had forced him to serve another term. The same problems—strong partisanship, diplomatic struggles with Europe, growing divisions over domestic policy—hindered the calm and unity Washington had sought since the first administration. The president longed to be at Mount Vernon with Martha in his declining years and wanted again to surrender the power the republic entrusted to him. Establishing the principle of rotation in office for the chief executive in a republic was also chiefly on his mind. In 1792, Washington told Madison, "The spirit of the government may render a rotation in the executive officers more congenial with their ideas of liberty and safety, that I take my leave of them as a public man."

The party divisions in the 1790s and Republican attacks on him led Washington to split with Madison and Jefferson. He naturally turned to Hamilton as his trusted ally of twenty-five years who knew his mind more than any other public figure to rewrite the address. The two had met in Philadelphia in February, when Hamilton was in the city arguing before the Supreme Court. Washington broached the subject of rewriting the Farewell, and Hamilton readily agreed. The president upheld the Union and national unity as the foundation of the republican government and wanted men from different political parties to be involved in the writing of the address as a measure of political harmony. He thought this would promote common republican political principles regardless of political affiliation when they saw the influence of their respective leaders. Therefore, in May, he sent Hamilton Madison's draft as well as some thoughts of his own as the basis of his composition.

Hamilton knew Washington's mind well. He had written Washington's correspondence during the war. The two shared the same political principles during the making and ratification of the Constitution. In the 1790s, they crafted American policies in the first presidency that created the nation. Hamilton was the best man for the job of expounding Washington's principled advice for the American people as the Father of His Country took his leave of public life forever. Hamilton spent the next few months intermittently working on the Farewell Address. He was to edit Madison's draft "if too verbose." Washington instructed Hamilton to write it to the American people in "honest, unaffected, simple garb." The Farewell was intended to be a practical guide to exercising American political principles rather than a philosophical treatise.

Washington was pleased with Hamilton's handiwork and sent it back after making a few alterations of his own. Hamilton suffered poor health and could not deliver additional edits as promised. The president made a few final stylistic changes and submitted it for publication. The Farewell Address was reflective of Hamilton's alliance with Washington for several years in war and peace. Washington was always his own man and the leading figure in the relationship, but depended on Hamilton to contribute his genius and play an indispensable role as Washington's main advisor. As historians Matthew Spalding and Patrick Garrity note, the making of the Farewell Address represents important themes in their lengthy collaboration and exemplified humility on Hamilton's part. "From the beginning, Hamilton understood himself as acting on Washington's instructions, following the president's intentions, and serving his purpose. Hamilton never claimed authorship or intimated publicly that his ideas were the ones reflected in the Address."[3]

Having written much of Washington's Farewell Address, Hamilton pivoted to electioneering for the Federalist Party in the first real contested presidential election in the new republic. Hamilton's primary object in the 1796 contest was to prevent the election of his partisan enemy, Thomas Jefferson, because of his political principles. He told a friend, "All personal and partial considerations must be discarded and everything must give way to the great object of excluding Jefferson."

The campaign caused a deep fissure in the ranks of Federalist leadership, especially between Hamilton and Vice President John Adams, Washington's heir apparent. Hamilton thought the vain and dyspeptic Adams was ill-suited temperamentally to the nation's highest office. Thomas Pinckney of South Carolina was a former governor who recently negotiated a highly favorable treaty with Spain opening the Mississippi River to American trade and had a character "far more discreet and conciliatory." Hamilton was mostly thinking strategically about the electoral map because Pinckney would win votes in the South as well as the Federalist stronghold in New England.

Adams was furious when he learned that Hamilton and other Federalists were campaigning for his rivals in the party. Jefferson even shrewdly sent him a letter intimating that Hamilton was engaging in political machinations to defeat Adams. "You may be cheated of your succession by a trick worthy the subtlety of your arch-friend in New York," Jefferson cautioned.

Adams generally took the bait, though during more lucid moments he understood that Hamilton was working for the strongest Federalist candidate rather than trying to keep him from the presidency. Nevertheless, Adams's disdain for Hamilton was mean-spirited and strongly xenophobic. Hamilton was "the bastard brat of a Scotch pedlar" or a "Creole bastard." His obscure origins were "not only contemptible but infamous." Adams even questioned his patriotism, arguing that the foreigner "could scarcely acquire the opinions, feelings, or principles of the American people." This was a strange opinion of Washington's wartime aide, the author of the *Federalist*, and the first treasury secretary whose patriotism and dedication to his adopted country was beyond dispute. Adams thought him "always pretending to morality but with as debauched morals as old Franklin." Adams contributed to a long-standing myth that Hamilton was a serial womanizer that is still popular today. In Adams's view, Hamilton had "a superabundance of secretions which he could not find whores enough to draw off," and "His fornications, adulteries, and his incests were propagated far and wide."

Adams narrowly won the presidency with seventy-one electoral votes to Jefferson's sixty-eight votes. Pinckney received fifty-nine votes, and Aaron Burr came in last with thirty votes. Because electors each exercised two ballots for president and vice president, the 1796 election resulted in the anomaly that candidates of different parties held the two offices. Hamilton was laid up with a leg injury as the results were announced but was satisfied with the fact that Jefferson had been defeated.

Adams somewhat foolishly kept Washington's cabinet in place rather than appointing his own men. Thomas Pickering was at State, Oliver Wolcott was at Treasury, and James McHenry was at War. They were all friends and associates of Hamilton who were to some degree influenced by him. Adams feared that they were Hamilton's dupes and controlled by him rather than loyalty to the president. This bred a great deal of distrust within the administration and created additional tension between the two. Hamilton expected to have the same influence with Adams as he had with Washington and sent the new president a lengthy missive with policy recommendations. Adams resented the advice because of its source and ignored it. Politics continued to have a strong attraction for Hamilton.

That summer, scurrilous journalist James Callender maliciously exposed Hamilton's affair with Maria Reynolds and turned it into a major sex scandal that had the potential to ruin Hamilton politically. The affair occurred back in 1791, but the nasty partisanship of the decade was dredged up to embarrass Hamilton. Callender most likely discovered his evidence from Republican intriguer and former clerk of the House of Representatives John Beckley, who in turn received it from James Monroe, one of the congressmen who had professed to be satisfied that the affair was only personal and involved no financial malfeasance at Treasury. Hamilton believed Monroe had shared the information with Callender. Hamilton confronted Monroe, exchanged personal insults, and the antagonists narrowly avoided fighting a duel.

Hamilton's reaction still largely confounds modern understanding. He wrote a lengthy pamphlet revealing every lurid detail of the affair. Readers from different political persuasions cringed when they read it and were astounded at the folly of publishing such a self-destructive exposé. As biographer Ron Chernow perceptively notes, the eighteenth-century understanding of honor provides some explanation. "He was prepared to sacrifice his private reputation to preserve his public honor."[4] Hamilton was willing to sacrifice himself, hurt the woman he loved, and destroy his marriage to preserve his public honor and the integrity of the financial institutions he had erected.

The Republicans were perplexed but delighted with Hamilton's disclosure. Callender gleefully noted that Hamilton had done more damage than "fifty of the best pens in America could have said against him." Eliza stoically stood by her husband despite the incalculable pain of his betrayal. She was even pregnant with their sixth child, William Stephen, and gave birth when the scandal broke. Hamilton was absent for the birth and the nearly fatal case of typhoid suffered by fifteen-year-old Philip. His personal life was in shambles, and his political future uncertain at best.

CHAPTER 19

QUASI-WAR WITH FRANCE (AND THE DEMOCRATIC-REPUBLICANS)

Foreign affairs drew Hamilton back into politics when serious diplomatic tensions arose with France. The Jay Treaty outraged the French, who interpreted the treaty as an Anglo-American alliance aimed at France. The five-member Directory that governed France used the treaty as a pretext for seizing American shipping around the West Indies and impressing American sailors. That spring, French privateers nabbed more than three hundred American vessels, violating American national sovereignty and neutral rights. The French government insulted the United States by refusing to meet with American minister Charles Cotesworth Pinckney. The French minister Pierre Auguste Adet even tried to sway the 1796 election toward the Democratic-Republicans because they were more favorably disposed to France. President Washington thought the French actions were "outrageous beyond conception."

Hamilton concurred that the French actions were shocking, but his foreign policy recommendations were moderate and conciliatory. Contrary to contemporary and historical assessments, Hamilton was not bent on war with a hated rival or trying to create a monarchist military state. Instead, he was primarily interested in preserving peace through strength and defending the national honor against depredations. This is somewhat remarkable considering his hatred of revolutionary France and its partisan American supporters.

Hamilton sensibly wanted to avoid war with France at all costs. "It is all important that the people should be satisfied that the government has made every exertion to avert rupture as early as possible," he told Washington. The United States was no more prepared to go to war with a major European power than it had been in 1793 or in 1795. Moreover, he feared an unsuccessful war would reverberate domestically, damaging the institutions he had painstakingly erected during the Washington administrations and thereby benefiting Jefferson's party. Still, the United States could not sit idly by while another country humiliated American national honor and violated its neutrality. He urged preparedness on the new president by proposing a naval force and a twenty-five-thousand-man provisional army. "My opinion is to exhaust the expedients of negotiation and at the same time to prepare vigorously for the worst," Hamilton told treasury secretary Oliver Wolcott. President John Adams largely adopted the same policy of preserving American neutrality through diplomacy and strength, but the two Federalist rivals somehow seemed at odds over foreign policy.

Hamilton suggested President Adams send a bipartisan, three-man commission to France to negotiate an end to the crisis. He even recommended that opposition leader James Madison join the commission to win Republican support for the mission. He shrewdly knew that if the French refused to entreat with the commission, they would show "in the most glaring light to our people her unreasonableness." It would also have the benefit "of refuting completely the charge that the actual administration desire war with France." Hamilton had learned valuable, sobering lessons from the Jay Treaty experience and applied them for the good of the country. However, the cabinet steadfastly refused to invite any Republicans to the mission, and the president refused to appear like he was Hamilton's puppet. For his part, partisanship guided Jefferson's rejection of the idea that a leading Republican would accept participating in successful peace negotiations that would strengthen the president and his rival party.

In the end, Adams expressed his independence by selecting John Marshall, Charles Cotesworth Pinckney, and Republican Elbridge Gerry.

In late March, President Adams called a special session of Congress for May to deal with the crisis. Hamilton praised the president for the course of action. "I believe there is no danger of want of firmness in the executive. If he is not ill-advised he will not want prudence. I mean to believe that he is himself disposed to a prudently firm course." Adams's speech was firm yet conciliatory. He warned that future provocations would be "repelled with a decision which shall convince France and the world that we are not a degraded people, humiliated under a colonial spirit of fear and sense of inferiority, fitted to be the miserable instruments of foreign influence, and regardless of national honor, character, and interest." The president called on Congress to raise a navy to protect American shipping, strengthen coastal defenses, and mobilize the militia.

The American commissioners endured their long voyage but did not receive a warm welcome in Paris. French foreign minister Charles Maurice de Talleyrand-Périgord used his position to enrich himself. Talleyrand received them briefly, but his agents carried out his avaricious instructions to make outrageous and insulting demands that the Americans were bound to decline. The French agents were known as X, Y, and Z in dispatches home. They demanded that President Adams disavow his bellicose speech to Congress. They also demanded that the United States immediately pay all outstanding loans owed to France, and in turn extend a massive loan of some thirteen million dollars to France. The agents insolently demanded that the Americans pay indemnification for the damage to their ships seized by French privateers. Finally, the French demanded a huge personal bribe as the cost of doing business with Talleyrand and meeting the insufferable French terms. Pinckney indignantly professed, "No! No! Not a sixpence!" Popular opinion altered his words into the slogan: "Millions for defense, but not one cent for tribute." This rallying cry animated the breasts of American patriots who would not submit their national honor to such humiliations.

In the wake of rumors about the outrageous demands, Hamilton spoke to Secretary of War McHenry about mobilizing for war with suggestions that looked much like Adams's from the previous May.

Hamilton argued for the arming of merchant vessels, the construction of a navy, and calling up twenty thousand regulars supplemented by a provisional army of thirty thousand.

When word finally reached the United States the following March 1798, Abigail Adams reported that the news "has been like an electrical shock." The president laid the dispatches before the House of Representatives in early April. The Republicans tried to turn the calamity into political advantage, but failed miserably. The country was gripped by war fever. Over the next few months, members of Congress shared popular outrage and authorized war preparations including arming merchant ships, building twelve frigates, and creating a Provisional Army of ten thousand and an Additional Army, though they did not declare war. The Congress also implemented a trade embargo against France, abrogated existing treaties, and authorized American vessels to attack predatory French ships. The Quasi-War with France was one of the first undeclared wars that Americans would fight. As historian George Herring notes, the "war scare of 1798 heightened already bitter divisions at home."[1]

The Quasi-War and creation of the army also fueled personal disputes within the administration among Federalists. Vanity superseded healthy policy deliberations when personalities and egos clashed. Hamilton and Adams were the primary combatants as their feud reached its zenith. Although they agreed on how to respond to French aggression, their mutual contempt divided the government during the crisis.

Once Congress authorized the creation of the expansion and mobilization of the army, President Adams had to choose a commander. As Hamilton informed Washington, there was a consensus that in the event of war the country would call on him to serve the republic once again. Washington was advancing in age and was reluctant to leave the repose of his retirement at Mount Vernon. Hamilton lobbied the general, warning him that he would be "compelled to make the sacrifice." Washington demurred and offered a compromise to fulfill his duty. His subordinates would raise, organize, and train the army, and he would not take the field unless there was a French invasion (which they saw as a real possibility).

Washington acceded to Adams's request to command the army, and he was symbolically approved by the Senate in time for the Fourth of July. However, Washington predicated his service on appointing his own generals. The demand rankled Adams, but he could hardly refuse. Adams had always dreamed of military glory and was now denied leadership even though he was commander-in-chief. The president was further annoyed when Hamilton presumptuously submitted his usual recommendations for organizing the army and preparing for war.

Washington conferred with McHenry and Pickering on the selection of generals. He expressed his great faith in Hamilton's incomparable administrative abilities. Hamilton's "services ought to be secured at almost any price." Washington's list of generals irritated Adams, who would be forced to accept his hated rival.

Washington selected Hamilton as the commander because of their mutual trust and vision shaping the American republic for more than twenty years. Moreover, Hamilton had invaluable experience as an aide during the war, which had allowed him to understand the needs of the entire army rather than just a war command. Washington praised Hamilton's character and abilities to the president with a final statement on Hamilton's indispensability: "That he is ambitious I readily grant, but it is of the laudable kind which prompts a man to excel in whatever he takes in hand. He is enterprising, quick in his perceptions, and his judgment intuitively great; qualities essential to a military character and therefore I repeat that his loss will be irreparable."

The surprising choice for next in command was South Carolinian Charles Cotesworth Pinckney. The southerner was selected because the expected French invasion would target Florida and Louisiana. Washington broke with military protocol in placing them ahead of Henry Knox, but the general's personal affection for Knox was unbroken after twenty years of friendship.

The list of officers was a bitter pill for Adams to swallow. "If I should consent to the appointment of Hamilton as a second in rank, I should consider it as the most irresponsible action of my whole life and the most difficult to justify. He is not a native of the United States, but a foreigner."

Over the next several months, Hamilton dedicated himself to creating a national army and managed the most minute details. He worked with Washington, McHenry, and Pickering on recruiting, supplies, regulations, and numerous other tasks. Secretary of War McHenry was unequal to the job, so Hamilton assumed even more responsibilities to ensure that everything was done right. Meanwhile, he served at considerable personal sacrifice financially due to the time spent away from his law practice. But he served his country patriotically and selflessly because the national security and honor were endangered by a foreign power, and especially the revolutionary nation he loathed.

His political enemies always suspected that Hamilton had dangerous intentions to use the army to overthrow the American republic and install himself as emperor. Hamilton certainly had larger objects in mind, but they were noble purposes. He supported a permanent military establishment to provide for the national defense of the United States. The distrust he acquired of militias during the war and the need for a permanent army persisted, even as Republicans clung to their antipathy to standing armies. Moreover, he had written President Washington's final annual message to Congress in which they had proposed a military academy to train an officer corps with a national outlook to bind the Union together. It was an "evident maxim of policy which requires every nation to be prepared for war while cultivating peace and warns it against suffering the military spirit and knowledge wholly to decay."

Another important strategic consideration in Hamilton's mind was the possibility of marching the army into Spanish-controlled Florida, Louisiana, and perhaps even Mexico and South America. Biographer Ron Chernow calls it "one of the most flagrant instances of poor judgment in Hamilton's career."[2] However, the idea may not have been that radical or hare-brained. Hamilton shared the common belief that Americans had a manifest destiny to settle the continent. He was fearful that European imperial diplomacy threatened American national security and made the United States a pawn of continental politics. He anticipated the Monroe Doctrine by suggesting that the United States should help liberate the Americas from European control and prevent the great powers from further interference. The proposed "enterprises [are] of great moment to the permanent interests of this country." He thought, "I have been long in the habit of considering the acquisition of those countries as essential to the permanency of the Union, which

I consider as very important to the welfare of the whole." These were not the words of a naked imperialist or a "second Bonaparte" (as Abigail Adams called him) but those of a shrewd strategic thinker. Indeed, French designs for an American empire became clear when they soon acquired Florida and Louisiana from Spain.

In December, the president dispatched a new minister to France to enter negotiations to repair the broken relationship. The move effectively decreased tensions and ended the war scare between the two countries. Hamilton supported a peaceful resolution to the Quasi-War, but thought the timing of Adams's announcement was obtuse. Talleyrand was out, the continental war was not going well, and the Directory was tottering. If the last decade of French history was any guide, a change of government—conceivably a dictatorship—was imminent. "The President has resolved to send the commissioners to France notwithstanding the change of affairs there," Hamilton told Washington. "All my calculations lead me to regret the measure." He thought it might be prudent to wait out events and angrily confronted the president over the measure in a Trenton boardinghouse.

Nevertheless, the president's gambit to send another mission to France peacefully resolved the Quasi-War. As Hamilton predicted, the French threat did not necessarily dissipate as evidenced by its acquisition of Spanish territory in North America the day after peace was secured with the American diplomats. Nevertheless, the object of peace that the two men shared had been achieved and averted a possibly disastrous war for the new nation. Hamilton soon complied with a congressional order to disband the army.

During the debates over preparing for war and the most honorable means of realizing peace with France, Congress fueled the political controversy by passing the Alien and Sedition Act in June and July of 1798. Neither Adams (who signed the bills) nor Hamilton urged the creation of the bills and were only lukewarm supporters. Indeed, Hamilton opposed early versions of the bills because he thought them too radical and dangerous to liberty. The Alien Act lengthened the period of naturalization and permitted the president to deport aliens who were considered a national security threat. Hamilton was an immigrant who should have been more sympathetic to opposing xenophobia than his comments indicate. "My opinion is that the mass [of foreigners] ought to be obliged to leave the country." But, he told Pickering, "Let us not be cruel or violent." He was concerned about French influence and their cozy relationship with Republicans during the Quasi-War, which was reasonable considering the machinations Hamilton witnessed of Genet, Adet, and others. The provisions of the Naturalization Act were never applied.

The Sedition Act made it a crime to speak or publish "false, scandalous, and malicious" writings against the president, Congress, or the U.S. government with the intent to "defame" or bring them into "contempt or disrepute." Therefore, it blatantly violated the First Amendment's protection of political speech criticizing the government. Hamilton thought that "There are provisions in this bill which according to a cursory view appear to me highly exceptionable and such as more than anything else may endanger civil war. . . . I hope sincerely the thing may not be hurried through. Let us not establish a tyranny. Energy is a very different thing from violence." He supported the liberal provision in the bill for truth as a defense in libel cases. He was also concerned that if the Federalists in Congress pushed too hard to shut down the Republican opposition, "we shall then give to faction body and solidity." Still, he could not contain his partisan feelings that the scurrilous, partisan editors were "in open contempt and defiance of the laws they are permitted to continue their destructive labors. Why are they not sent away? Are laws of this kind passed merely to excite odium and remain a dead letter?" The administration executed the law and prosecuted twenty newspaper editors, which had a chilling effect on a free press during the war fever.

Jefferson and Madison's response was to develop extraconstitutional doctrines in the Kentucky and Virginia Resolutions, respectively. In the Virginia Resolution, Madison advanced the idea that the states could "interpose" themselves against an unconstitutional federal law, though it was left vague as to exactly what constituted that doctrine. More radically, in the Kentucky Resolution, Jefferson argued that the states could "nullify" federal law. Hamilton characterized nullification as a dangerous "gangrene" and believed it was the logical fulfillment of a decade of Republican anticentralist thinking. He thought that the resolutions were a "regular conspiracy to overturn the government" and questioned their loyalty in the same way that they charged Hamilton with monarchism. In the highly charged partisan atmosphere, Hamilton believed the Republicans posed a potential threat to national security and pondered the use of a show of force to avert a rebellion. He never marched the army through Virginia as contemplated, and the resolutions were more peacefully rejected by the legislatures of ten states who did not believe them sound constitutional thinking.

When growing numbers of Pennsylvanians protested the tax to raise an army in the Quasi-War, Hamilton's fears of domestic rebellion seemed justified. With the Whiskey Rebellion in mind, Hamilton thought that the administration should quell the growing rebellion decisively before it grew into a full-blown insurrection. An inadequate force showing feebleness would only encourage the rebels. Hamilton sent a combined force of federal troops and militia into eastern Pennsylvania, where they dispersed the rebels and arrested the ringleaders. Following the precedent of the Whiskey Rebellion, President Adams pardoned those who were convicted of treason.

Peace eventually calmed most of these domestic partisan tensions, at least for a time. In late 1799, Washington died of a throat ailment, sending Hamilton and the entire country into mourning. On December 26, Hamilton marched in a funeral procession from Congress Hall to the German Lutheran Church in Philadelphia. "Light-Horse" Harry Lee delivered his famous eulogy, praising Washington as "first in war, first in peace, first in the hearts of his countrymen." Hamilton was crushed and lost his friend, mentor, and political ally since the Revolutionary War. "Perhaps no friend of his has more cause to lament on personal account than myself. . . . My imagination is gloomy, my heart sad," he told a mutual friend. "I have been much indebted to the kindness of the general. . . . He was an aegis very essential to me." He sent Martha a consoling and touching letter to assuage her grief. Hamilton lost not only a friend and mentor, but a figure who provided guidance and somewhat of a moderating influence.

CHAPTER 20

THE ELECTION OF 1800 AND THE RETREAT FROM POLITICS

The election of 1800 drew Hamilton into a heightened partisan war almost like any other in American history. Hamilton was caught in this political maelstrom and engaged in imprudent and even self-destructive actions. His political compass was off and caused several blunders in the election.

In the spring of 1800, Hamilton campaigned hard for a Federalist slate in New York City. He politicked from morning to night and routinely skipped meals. The election for the state assembly was critically important because that body cast the state's votes in the electoral college. Hamilton thought he had a winning idea that would tap into the Republican base. He developed a slate of candidates for New York City that was supposed to appeal to a mass audience because it was made up of political unknowns, including artisans. The Republicans, on the other hand, outmaneuvered Hamilton and selected a group of well-known politicos such as former Governor George Clinton and war hero Horatio Gates.

The Hamiltonian strategy completely backfired, and the Republicans swept the New York City seats, which had typically been securely Federalist. A panicked Hamilton and some of his fellow party members met hastily to discuss how to proceed. The Federalists present decided that they had no choice but to engineer a different outcome to overturn their electoral drubbing. The proposal was to call a special session of the legislature to change the election laws after the fact, relinquishing legislative control over the electors in favor of a popular election. Hamilton related the manipulative scheme to his friend and governor, John Jay.

Hamilton endorsed the measure because he feared the consequences of his arch political nemesis winning the election. The prospect led to some hyperbole. Jefferson was, in Hamilton's opinion, "an *atheist* in religion and a *fanatic in politics.*" His election might lead to "the overthrow of the government by stripping it of its due energies . . . a revolution after the manner of Bonaparte." Therefore, Hamilton advised the governor that, "In times like these . . . it will not do to be overscrupulous. It is easy to sacrifice the substantial interests of society by a strict adherence to ordinary rules." No action was taken on his extraordinary proposal, and the election results stood. Jefferson won New York.

That spring and summer of 1800, Hamilton fought enemies on every side, including within his own Federalist party. The mutual contempt Hamilton and Adams had for each other peaked when Adams finally purged his cabinet of Secretary of War McHenry and Secretary of State Pickering after four years. Adams correctly believed that they were loyal to Hamilton and sought to put his own men in office. Hamilton thought Adams mad and resolved to break with his party and oppose Adams's election "even though the consequence should be the election of *Jefferson.*"

Hamilton kept his promise and wrote a lengthy missive about Adams's character flaws that made him temperamentally unsuited to be reelected. Adams was unstable and suffered an inability to govern his passions. The letter was intended to circulate only among selected Federalist allies, but it is difficult to understand how Hamilton could not have conceived that it might get into the wrong hands. After it was leaked to the press, Hamilton published it as a fifty-four-page pamphlet publicly assassinating Adams's character and unfitness for office. The Republicans were gleeful, and Madison congratulated Jefferson on its publication. Federalist Fisher Adams thought that it was the best piece Hamilton had ever written—and absolutely devastating for the party.

As if the pamphlet were not enough, Hamilton and Adams continued their personal feud. Hamilton felt that the president had assailed his honor in charging him with being the leader of a "*British faction.*" Only a month before the election, Hamilton demanded satisfaction of the allegations that were "a base, wicked, cruel calumny, destitute even of a plausible pretext to excuse the folly or mask the depravity which must have dictated it." Fortunately, the sitting president was not tempted to fight a duel while in office.

In the end, Jefferson tied Aaron Burr with seventy-three votes each, and the election went to the House of Representatives. Hamilton continued to work behind the scenes, but his maneuvers now assumed a statesmanlike, principled approach. Hamilton had long known and worked with Burr and thought him the most unprincipled, self-interested politician who lusted for office to satisfy his own ambitions rather than serving the republic. In a withering critique of Burr, Hamilton asserted: "He is bankrupt beyond redemption, except by the plunder of his country. His public principles have no other spring or aim than his own aggrandizement. . . . If he can, he will certainly disturb our institutions to secure to himself *permanent* power and with it *wealth.* His is truly the *Catiline* of America." Burr would also disgrace the country abroad and damage the national honor. On the other hand, Hamilton had battled Jefferson politically for a decade and endured any number of accusations of monarchism, but he believed that the Virginian had a good character and could be trusted with the presidency. "If there be a man in the world I ought to hate it is Jefferson," he explained. "With Burr I have always been personally well, but the public good must be paramount to every private consideration."

Hamilton lobbied hard for James Bayard of Delaware to give his crucial vote to Jefferson, and that state did swing for Jefferson in the House and made him the third president. The conciliatory vision and policy directions in Jefferson's inaugural address pleased Hamilton, who thought that Jefferson had retracted his earlier opposition to Hamilton's financial system and would preserve it. Once in office, Jefferson did instruct Treasury Secretary Albert Gallatin to comb through treasury records for evidence of Hamilton's malfeasance. Gallatin found nothing and was instead struck by the elegance of "the most perfect system ever formed."

After the furies of the election had calmed, Hamilton seemed to take stock of his life. He progressively desired the simple pleasures of home and family, and mostly left the party wars of the 1790s behind. It was not simply the decisive victory of Jefferson that drove Hamilton from public life. In his midforties, he had time to reflect on his life and dedicated himself to domestic felicity.

Hamilton shared with his beloved Eliza his longing to focus more on family, home, and career. He reflected: "It is absolutely necessary to me when absent to hear frequently of you and my dear children. While all other passions decline in me, those of love and friendship gain new strength. It will be more and more my endeavor to abstract myself from all pursuits which interfere with those of affection. 'Tis here only I can find true pleasure."

To achieve his dream of domestic bliss, Hamilton purchased several acres of land north of downtown Manhattan with idyllic views of both the Harlem and Hudson Rivers. On this spot, he built a spacious home called the Grange for his large family, where they moved in 1802. While he continued to practice law in the city and dabble in public affairs, he found refuge from worldly cares in his home and garden.

Hamilton could not entirely keep his hand out of politics. He started the *New York Evening Post*, edited by a young lawyer, William Coleman. Like most newspapers of the time, the *Post* had a partisan angle and supported Federalist ideas. Hamilton had a lot of say over editorial content and contributed several essays. He penned essays arguing the Jeffersonians were destroying an independent judiciary with the repeal of the 1801 Judiciary Act. He was obviously at odds with the Jeffersonian governing philosophy, but was not blinded by ideology. He praised the Louisiana Purchase as an important acquisition for the good of the country and constitutionally sanctioned. Still, he did not write with the same fervor that drove his defenses of domestic and foreign policies of the Washington administrations, and the personal and political battles of the later 1790s.

Hamilton had even more cause to retreat from politics to the comforts of family when his eldest son, Philip, was killed in a duel. In late November 1801, the nineteen-year-old aspiring lawyer exchanged heated words and insults with a young Republican lawyer, George Eacker, at a theater. Philip was still fuming over a Fourth of

July oration in which Eacker had accused the elder Hamilton of using the army for political ends. Eacker endured some insults and then called Philip and his friend rascals. The intricacies of the code duello were quickly followed by the hot-headed rivals. Eacker first fought an inconclusive duel with the friend and then with Philip.

Young Hamilton and Eacker met at Weehawken. Hamilton's father had advised him to withhold his shot, though Eacker did not have the same compunction and shot Philip in the hip. Philip was carried to the Church home and placed under the care of Dr. David Hosack. Hamilton was so distraught upon hearing the news that he suffered fainting spells. He and Betsy were hysterical as they watched their son die after fourteen hours of great pain. Their daughter Angelica was driven insane by the loss of her brother and lived in denial that he was dead for the rest of her life.

Hamilton sank into a deep depression as a result of his beloved Philip's death. He shared his grief with his trusted friend, Gouverneur Morris. The pain of the bereaved father was "beyond comparison the most afflicting of my life. . . . He was truly a fine youth." He was disconsolate for months. He tried to remain stoic in face of the tragedy and take a Christian perspective on death. "My loss is indeed great. But why should I repine? It was the will of heaven, and he is now out of the reach of the seductions and calamities of a world full of folly, full of vice, full of danger, of least value in proportion as it is best known. I firmly trust also that he has safely reached the haven of eternal of repose and felicity."

But Hamilton had outlived his son and was heartbroken. His despair was plainly still evident months later and spilled over into a gloomy reflection about America and his role in the experiment. "Mine is an odd destiny. Perhaps no man in the United States has sacrificed or done more for the present Constitution than myself. . . . I am still laboring to prop the frail and worthless fabric. Yet I have the murmur of its friends no less than the curses of its foes for my rewards. What can I do better than withdraw from the scene?" he wrote Gouverneur Morris in February 1802. "Every day proves to me more and more, that this American world was not made for me."

Hamilton gradually recovered and started thinking about politics again. Philip's death caused him to think more about his Christian faith and how it could promote a healthy American regime. The fruit of his deliberation was a Christian Constitutional Society.

The society would counter the influence of Jeffersonian ideals in the Democratic-Republican Party. The Federalists believed that these principles were based upon atheism and moral license. While biographer Ron Chernow calls it an "execrable idea" and a "retrograde" notion because it saw a role for religion in the public square, it accorded with the constitutional principles of many founders and citizens at the time.[1]

Hamilton's idea was consistent with a national civil religion rather than an established church. The society would promote religion, and specifically Christianity, in American politics and civic life to support virtuous citizens and politics in the constitutional republic. Moreover, the society would give churchgoing Christians a place to discuss politics and build an organization that advanced their vision of an enduring republic. This combination of faith and reason, constitutionalism and religion was especially necessary in Hamilton's mind not merely because of the Jeffersonians but a world in flames because of the secular, utopian visions of the French Revolution. He wrote:

> Nothing is more fallacious than to expect to produce any valuable or permanent results, in political projects, by relying merely on the reason of men. . . . For at the very moment [the Democratic-Republicans] are eulogizing the reason of men and professing to appeal only to that faculty, they are courting the strongest and most active passion of the human heart—VANITY! It is no less true that the Federalists seem not to have attended to the fact sufficiently; and that they erred in relying so much on the rectitude and utility of their measures, as to have neglected the cultivation of popular favor by fair and justifiable expedients. . . . In my opinion the present Constitution is the standard to which we are to cling. Under its banners, bona fide must we combat our political foes—rejecting all changes but through the channel itself provides for amendments.

Hamilton's proposal was reflective of a strengthening personal Christian faith especially as he thought about mortality in the wake of Philip's death. He and Eliza rented a pew at Trinity Church. Bible reading and prayer became an increasingly important part of his daily routine. When his mother-in-law passed away, Hamilton advised his wife to meet the tragedy with "Christian fortitude." He welcomed the solace that only religion could give in his contemplative moments at the Grange.

Hamilton had had his share of political frustrations over the past few years. At times, he lost his way without the guiding hand of Washington. In 1804, he seemed like his former self in articulating American political principles. Harry Croswell was the editor of the periodical the *Wasp* who wrote that President Jefferson was hostile to the Constitution and that James Callender grossly slandered members of the Federalist Party. The chief architect of the opposition to the Alien and Sedition Acts, Jefferson stated that a few public prosecutions of Federalist editors "would have a wholesome effect in restoring the integrity of the presses." The Jeffersonians prosecuted Croswell and convicted him. Hamilton took Croswell on as a client, and defended the freedom of the press and the right to criticize government officials.

In the trial, Hamilton warned that the United States had to support the principle of rotation in office. Each party could not persecute the other when it came to power. A free press was a guardian of liberty against oppressive government. It gave the American people "early alarm and put us on our guard against the encroachments of power. This then is a right of the utmost importance, one for which, instead of yielding it up, we ought rather to spill our blood." Tyranny would not be introduced by force of arms, Hamilton predicted, but by destroying "a popular spirit of enquiry." Liberty was "subverted only by a pretense of adhering to all the forms of law, and yet by breaking down the substance of our liberties." The principle of liberty of the press "consists, in my idea, in publishing the truth from good motives and for justifiable ends, though it reflect on the government, on magistrates, or individuals." Any abuse of this principle was contrary to the spirit of constitutional republican government.

Hamilton again defended truth in libel cases as he did when the Alien and Sedition Acts were passed. Truth led a reasonable person to "infer that there was no design to injure another." He said, "I never did think the truth was a crime. I am glad the day is come in which it is to be decided, for my soul has ever abhorred the thought that a free man dared not speak the truth." Nevertheless, the judge instructed the jury to consider only the facts not the truth or intentions. The jury found Croswell guilty despite Hamilton's reasoned plea for a free press. Croswell was initially denied a new trial but was granted it when the state legislature passed a new law that allowed truth as a defense in libel cases.

Hamilton was only forty-seven years old in early 1804, but he had been involved in public affairs since he was twenty. The constant battling of political opponents had lost much of its former charm for him. He had found solitude with his beloved family at a home that served as a retreat even from the whirligig of politics and finance of New York City. He may have looked forward to relative peace in his twilight years, with his hand only loosely in politics, but it was not to be.

CHAPTER 21

THE DUEL

Hamilton had lived according to a code of honor his entire life. He closely guarded his reputation and manhood from any disparagement. Most duels were satisfied and never fought, or were settled in a nonlethal exchange of gunfire. Hamilton had experienced many such threatening episodes that never reached the dueling grounds. But he had always been prepared to defend his honor should he be pressed to take the field.

Recently, however, Hamilton had had a change of heart. Philip's death by dueling ruined Hamilton's life and led him to adopt a great antipathy against the practice. He thought it violated the natural law and was morally wrong. Dueling was vindictive justice and offended the rule of law. In February, he argued in court that duels were wrong "on the principles of natural justice, that no man shall be the avenger of his own wrongs, especially by a deed, alike interdicted by the laws of God and of man."

Two months later, an Albany newspaper recounted a dinner party conversation that Hamilton attended. He reportedly impugned Burr's character and insulted his honor by calling him "a dangerous man and one who ought not be trusted." As if that were not enough, Hamilton maintained that he held "a still more despicable opinion."

Hamilton and Burr knew each other well, for they had faced off in court and sometimes worked together, representing the same client. They were jointly involved in New York and national politics over the past couple of decades, and their politics had taken a more personal turn recently. Hamilton had openly campaigned for Jefferson over Burr when the 1800 election went to the House of Representatives, and Burr published Hamilton's letter against Adams. Hamilton would support Burr's rival in the 1804 New York gubernatorial race that spring.

Hamilton's poor opinion of Burr was not a secret. Hamilton thought Burr was an unprincipled, scheming politician whose ambition for power seemed corrupt. Burr was not a patriotic servant of his country and the public good; rather, Burr seemed always to be serving his own interests. Hamilton's previous comment that Burr was an "embryo-Caesar" captures the disdain and fear he had for Burr's character.

Burr later commented that, "It is too well known that General Hamilton had long indulged himself in illiberal freedoms with my character. He had a peculiar talent of saying things improper and offensive." When he learned of the dinner party comments, Burr clearly had had enough of Hamilton playing fast and loose with his character. In June, Burr sent Hamilton a letter demanding an explanation. The two exchanged letters demanding satisfaction according to the code of honor, with Burr expecting a retraction that never came. Burr complained that he had endured "base slanders" for years and had exercised "forbearance till it approached humiliation." Neither backed down, leading to Hamilton's first duel.

Hamilton faced his mortality with resignation as he prepared a will and wrote letters to his dear wife. He explained to her that he wanted to avoid the duel, but "it was not possible, without sacrifices which would have rendered me unworthy of your esteem" because he would have earned a reputation as an unmanly coward. He also importantly revealed his intent in the coming duel.

The evidence is strong that the loss of his son, his stated opposition to dueling, and Hamilton's growing Christian faith led him to plan to throw away his shot. Hamilton told Eliza, "The scruples of a Christian have determined me to expose my own life to any extent, rather than subject myself to the guilt of taking the life of another. This much increases my hazards, and redoubles my pangs for you. But you had rather I should die innocent than life guilty." He then bid adieu to his "darling, darling wife." The day before the duel, his second, Nathaniel

Pendleton, fruitlessly tried to dissuade him from wasting his shot. He was hardly alone in planning to miss his opponent. Most duels ended with shots being exchanged to settle the affair and satisfy honor in a nonlethal manner.

Even with much on his mind on the night before the duel, Hamilton still thought of the health of the national Union. He wrote a Massachusetts Federalist, rebuking talk of secession coming from New England. "The result must be destructive to the present Constitution and eventually the establishment of separate governments framed on principles in their nature hostile to civil liberty."

In the early hours of July 11, 1804, Hamilton, Burr, and their seconds rowed across the Hudson to Weehawken, New Jersey, for the appointed duel. Dr. David Hosack was present in case one or both of the duelists were injured. The two grabbed a pistol and then walked to their assigned places ten paces from each other. Hamilton faced the rising morning sun. Pendleton issued the command, "Present."

The opponents lifted their pistols and fired simultaneously, with Hamilton's errant shot hitting the limb of a nearby tree. However, Burr's shot struck Hamilton in the abdomen, and he collapsed, clutching at the wound. The bullet had ripped through his liver and diaphragm, lodging in his spine. Burr apparently moved to assist Hamilton, but his second, William Van Ness, whisked him away from the scene and rowed off.

Nathaniel Pendleton attended to Hamilton while Dr. Hosack rushed to the site. Hamilton saw him and said, "This is a mortal wound, doctor," and slipped into unconsciousness. They carried him to the boat and transported him to William Bayard's mansion for medical attention. The doctor administered laudanum to relieve Hamilton's agonizing pain, but there was nothing he could do.

Hamilton knew that he was dying, and, when he regained consciousness, asked to take communion. Episcopal Bishop Right Reverend Benjamin Moore of Trinity Church hesitated to answer the summons because of the nature of the incident. Instead, a Scottish Presbyterian pastor, Reverend John Mason, came to Hamilton, who renounced dueling and confessed his Christian faith. Later that day, Bishop Moore reconsidered and administered communion after Hamilton reiterated his opposition to dueling and his Christian beliefs.

No one wanted to relay the tragic news to Eliza, who was at home at the Grange. Finally, Eliza was summoned and went to him, thinking it was a relatively insignificant ailment. However, she became hysterical when she discovered the truth. Eliza went to her dying husband to console him. He advised her to bear up and remember that she was a Christian in the face of death. Their children also came to visit their father and say goodbye. Alexander Hamilton died the following afternoon.

The funeral was held on Saturday, July 14. Shops closed, ships in the harbor flew their flags at half-mast, and church bells rang. Thousands of New Yorkers came out to witness the funeral procession of their favorite son in a mahogany coffin adorned with a sword and hat on its slow march to Trinity Church. The affecting scene was "enough to melt a monument of marble" in the words of one observer.

Hamilton's good friend, Gouverneur Morris, delivered the eulogy. He recited Hamilton's heroic exploits in the Revolutionary War, his Constitution-making, and his political contributions. Most important, Morris praised Hamilton's "strenuous . . . unremitting . . . efforts to establish and to preserve the Constitution."

EPILOGUE

Alexander Hamilton has been used and misused, becoming many things to many people throughout American history, as historian Stephen Knott has brilliantly demonstrated.[1] The recent resurgence in Hamilton's popularity has again rendered this founding father a pawn in the social and political battles of the day, and perhaps revealed more about his progressive and conservative interpreters than about Hamilton. He remains as controversial in death as he was in life.

Hamilton is the most wildly popular founding father at present. While some scholars may continue to lament that Hamilton's popularity is part of the continuing "founders' chic" that has restored interest in the founding fathers via best-selling books by David McCullough or Joseph Ellis, television miniseries, and even plays that are rapped, I think it is a very good trend. More young people and citizens have become very interested in the American founding, its principles, and its personalities. It is not hard to understand the interest in our nation's heritage or the attraction to one of its most important, yet previously underappreciated, founders.

Hamilton's life was deeply staked on the American experiment in liberty and self-government. He served his country in its War for Independence, advocated a political philosophy entrenched in its republican ideals, dedicated his life to public service in numerous capacities, and acted as a lawgiver giving shape to the regime of liberty and its institutions. Hamilton may not have a massive monument honoring his achievements on the National Mall, but his monument is all around us in the enduring constitutional republic and free-enterprise capitalist economy.

CHRONOLOGY

January 11, 1757: Alexander Hamilton was born

1768: Hamilton's mother died

1773: Hamilton arrived in New York

1774: Hamilton wrote the pamphlet *A Full Vindication of the Measures of Congress*

1775: The New York Provincial Congress appointed Hamilton captain of the artillery

Hamilton wrote the *Farmer Refuted* pamphlet

1776: Battle of New York

The Declaration of Independence was adopted

Battle of Trenton

1777: Battle of Princeton

Washington invited Hamilton to serve as an aide-de-camp as a lieutenant colonel

Battle of Brandywine

Battle of Germantown

Battle of Saratoga

1778: The winter at Valley Forge

Battle of Monmouth Courthouse

1780: Benedict Arnold's traitorous plot revealed

Hamilton married Elizabeth Schuyler

1781: Hamilton resigned from Washington's staff after a falling out

Battle of Yorktown

Hamilton wrote the *Continentalist* essays

1782: Hamilton was admitted to the New York Bar

Hamilton was elected to the Continental Congress from New York

Friend John Laurens was killed in battle

1783: The Newburgh Conspiracy

Hamilton opened his law office in New York

Peace Treaty with Great Britain ended the Revolutionary War

1784: Hamilton wrote *Letter from Phocion*

Rutgers v. Waddington (1784)

1785: Hamilton joined the New York Society for Promoting the Manumission of Slaves

1786: Hamilton attended the Annapolis Convention

1787: Hamilton attended the Constitutional Convention

1787–1788: Hamilton wrote fifty-one *Federalist* essays

1788: Hamilton attended the New York Ratifying Convention

1789: Hamilton was appointed secretary of the treasury in the Washington administration

1790: Hamilton submitted his *Report on Public Credit* to Congress

Hamilton submitted his *Report on a National Bank* to Congress

1791:   Hamilton wrote an opinion on the national bank defending its constitutionality

Hamilton had an affair with Maria Reynolds

Hamilton submitted his *Report on Manufactures* to Congress

1793:   Hamilton wrote the Pacificus essays defending Washington's Proclamation of Neutrality

1794:   Hamilton led the army to suppress the Whiskey Rebellion

1795:   The Senate ratified the Jay Treaty

Hamilton defended the Jay Treaty in the *Defense* essays

Hamilton resigned as secretary of the treasury

1796:   Hamilton helped Washington draft his Farewell Address

1797:   Hamilton published the Reynolds pamphlet detailing their affair

1798:   Hamilton was appointed inspector general of the army during the Quasi-War with France

1799:   George Washington died

1800:   Hamilton's *Letter Concerning the Public Conduct and Character of John Adams* was published

U.S. presidential election

1801:   Philip Hamilton was killed in a duel

1802:   Hamilton started the Christian Constitutional Society

1803:   Louisiana Purchase

July 11, 1804: Hamilton was shot in a duel with Aaron Burr and died the following day

BIBLIOGRAPHIC ESSAY

There is a growing list of excellent books on Alexander Hamilton, the Revolutionary War, the American founding, and the contentious new republic. This is a selected list of books that I found most helpful in my research.

There are several essential published collections of primary sources. Every scholar will naturally turn to Harold C. Syrett et al., *The Papers of Alexander Hamilton*, 27 vols. (Columbia University Press, 1961–1987). But the more casual reader will enjoy reading the letters and public writings of Hamilton in Joanne B. Freeman, ed., *Alexander Hamilton: Writings* (Library of America, 2001), and an abridged version by the same author, *The Essential Hamilton: Letters & Other Writings* (Library of America, 2017). An excellent brief collection of Hamilton's Revolutionary War public essays can be found in Richard B. Vernier, ed., *The Revolutionary Writings of Alexander Hamilton* (Liberty Fund, 2008). Carson Holloway and Bradford P. Wilson's forthcoming two-volume set of the *Political Writings of Alexander Hamilton* (Cambridge University Press, 2017) will prove to be an indispensable resource for scholars.

Several historians and biographers have written the standard books on Hamilton's life. Ron Chernow's magisterial *Alexander Hamilton* (Penguin, 2004), Forrest McDonald's *Alexander Hamilton: A Biography* (Norton, 1979), and Richard Brookhiser's *Alexander Hamilton, American* (Simon & Schuster, 1999), have laid the foundation for modern Hamilton scholarship. Other worthwhile biographies include Jacob Ernest Cooke, *Alexander Hamilton* (Charles Scribner's Sons, 1982), James Thomas Flexner, *The Young Hamilton: A Biography* (Little, Brown, 1978), John C. Miller, *Alexander Hamilton and the Growth of the New Nation* (Harper and Row, 1964), Broadus Mitchell, *Alexander Hamilton: Youth to Maturity, 1755-1788* (Macmillan, 1957), and *Alexander Hamilton: The National Adventure, 1788–1804* (Macmillan, 1962).

Hamilton's political philosophy has been scrutinized by several political scientists and historians. The best volume is the contribution by Karl-Friedrich Walling, *Republican Empire: Alexander Hamilton on War and Free Government* (University Press of Kansas, 1999), to the outstanding American Political Thought series. Other noteworthy additions include Gerald Stourzh, *Alexander Hamilton and the Idea of Republican Government* (Stanford University Press, 1970), and Michael P. Federici, *The Political Philosophy of Alexander Hamilton* (Johns Hopkins University Press, 2012), in another excellent series, The Political Philosophy of the American Founders, edited by Garrett Ward Sheldon. An older, useful work is Clinton Rossiter, *Alexander Hamilton and the Constitution* (Harcourt, Brace, and World, 1964). Stephen F. Knott has produced a remarkable volume on Hamilton's shifting place in American memory while clearing up numerous myths about the man in *Alexander Hamilton and the Persistence of Myth* (University Press of Kansas, 2002), also in the American Political Thought series.

Many books focus on Hamilton and his relationship with other founders. Stephen F. Knott and Tony Williams, *Washington & Hamilton: The Alliance That Forged America* (Sourcebooks, 2015), argues that it was the indispensable relationship of the American founding. Carson Holloway's *Hamilton versus Jefferson in the Washington Administration* (Cambridge, 2015) is a masterpiece of scholarship. John Ferling takes a strong anti-Hamiltonian stance in his book, *Jefferson and Hamilton: The Rivalry That Forged a Nation* (Bloomsbury, 2013). A useful collection of documents is contained in Noble E. Cunningham Jr., *Jefferson vs. Hamilton: Confrontations That Shaped a Nation* (Bedford, 2000). The relevant sections in David O. Stewart, *Madison's Gift: Five Partnerships That Built America* (Simon & Schuster, 2015), and the forthcoming Jay Cost, *The Price of Greatness: Alexander Hamilton, James Madison, and the Creation of American Oligarchy,* brilliantly examine the on-again, off-again relationship with James Madison that supplant other works on their relationship, including Michael I. Meyerson, *Liberty's Blueprint: How Madison and Hamilton Wrote the Federalist Papers, Defined the Constitution, and Made Democracy Safe for the World* (Basic, 2008) and Richard B. Morris, *Witnesses at the Creation: Hamilton, Madison, Jay, and the Constitution* (Holt Rinehart, 1985). Other outstanding books include Jack Rakove, *Revolutionaries: A New History of the Invention of America* (Houghton Mifflin, 2010), Gordon Wood, *Revolutionary Characters: What Made the Founders Different* (Penguin, 2006), Darren Staloff, *Hamilton, Adams, Jefferson: The Politics of Enlightenment and the American Founding,* and Joseph J. Ellis, *The Quartet: Orchestrating the Second American Revolution* (Knopf, 2015).

Historians have plumbed the depths of Hamilton's policies, including diplomatic historians who have scrutinized Hamilton's foreign policy. The best is John Lamberton Harper, *American Machiavelli: Alexander Hamilton and the Origins of U.S. Foreign Policy* (Cambridge, 2004). Another valuable addition is Lawrence S. Kaplan, *Alexander Hamilton: Ambivalent Anglophile* (Rowman & Littlefield, 2001). A magisterial overview of American foreign policy is George C. Herring, *From Colony to Superpower: U.S. Foreign Relations Since 1776* (Oxford University Press, 2008), in the Oxford History of the United States series. A highly enjoyable and readable book about Hamilton's economic policies is by business historian Thomas McCraw, *The Founders and Finance: How Hamilton, Gallatin, and Other Immigrants Forged a New Economy* (Harvard University Press, 2012). Two overviews of the American economy and national debt that discuss Hamilton's financial plans by economic historian John Steele Gordon are *Hamilton's Blessing: The Extraordinary Life and Times of Our National Debt* (Walker, 1997) and the same author's *An Empire of Wealth: The Epic History of American Economic Power.* Two outstanding books on Hamilton and the rule of law are Kate Elizabeth Brown, *Alexander Hamilton and the Development of American Law* (University Press of Kansas, 2017) and Peter Charles Hoffer, *Rutgers v. Waddington: Alexander Hamilton, the End of the War for Independence, and the Origins of Judicial Review* (University Press of Kansas) in the remarkable Landmark Law Cases and American Society series.

Many sources were instrumental to my interpretations of Hamilton's times. For the Caribbean, Richard S. Dunn, *Sugar and Slaves: The Rise of the Planter Class in the English West Indies, 1624-1713* (University of North Carolina Press, 2000), is a classic. Andrew Jackson O'Shaughnessy, *An Empire Divided: The American Revolution and the British Caribbean* (University of Pennsylvania Press, 2000) and *Matthew Parker, The Sugar Barons: Family, Corruption, Empire, and War in the West Indies* (Walker, 2011) were very useful. On New York in the American Revolution, Edward Countryman, *A People in Revolution: The American Revolution and Political Society in New York, 1760-1790* (Norton, 1989), and Richard M. Ketchum, *Divided Loyalties: How the American Revolution Came to New York* (Henry Holt, 2003).

The standard general studies of the Revolutionary War include Robert Middlekauff, *The Glorious Cause: The American Revolution, 1763-1789* (Oxford University Press, 1982), in the Oxford History of the United States series, and John Ferling, *Almost a Miracle: The American Victory in the War of Independence* (Oxford University Press, 2007). Specific studies of key battles and events involving Hamilton are Barnet Schechter, *The Battle for New York: The City at the Heart of the American Revolution* (Penguin, 2003), David Hackett Fischer, *Washington's Crossing* (Oxford University Press, 2004), in the Pivotal Moments series, David McCullough, *1776* (Simon & Schuster, 2005), Stephen R. Taaffe, *The Philadelphia Campaign, 1777-1778* (University Press of Kansas, 2003), in the Modern War Studies series, Richard M. Ketchum, *Saratoga: Turning Point of America's Revolutionary War* (Henry Holt, 1999), Paul Lockhart, *The Drillmaster of Valley Forge: The Baron de Steuben and the Making of the American Army* (Harper, 2008), Wayne Bodle, *The Valley Forge Winter: Civilians and Soldiers in War* (Penn State University Press, 2004), Nathaniel Philbrick, *Valiant Ambition: George Washington, Benedict Arnold, and the Fate of the American Revolution* (Penguin, 2016), and Richard M. Ketchum, *Victory at Yorktown: The Campaign That Won the Revolution* (Henry Holt, 2004). Two books on the dismal American war effort are Charles Royster, *A Revolutionary People at War: The Continental Army and American Character, 1775-1783* (University of North Carolina Press, 1996), and E. Wayne Carp, *To Starve the Army at Pleasure: Continental Army Administration and American Political Culture* (University of

North Carolina Press, 2004). The chapters in *Richard Kohn, Eagle and Sword: The Federalists and the Creation of the Military Establishment in America, 1783-1802* (Free Press, 1975) remains the best source on the Newburgh Conspiracy.

Books on the American founding and Constitution-making are numerous and growing rapidly. The most relevant to my research included Forrest McDonald, *Novus Ordo Seclorum: The Intellectual Origins of the Constitution* (University Press of Kansas, 1985), Richard Beeman, *Plain, Honest Men: The Making of the U.S. Constitution* (Random House, 2009), Pauline Meier, *Ratification: The People Debate the Constitution, 1787-1788* (Simon & Schuster, 2010), Jack Rakove, *Original Meanings: Politics and Ideas in the Making of the Constitution* (Vintage, 1996), and Max M. Edling, *A Revolution in Favor of Government: Origins of the U.S. Constitution and the Making of the American State* (Oxford University Press, 2003).

General studies of the divisive 1790s, the creation of the Hamiltonian system, and the rise of the new nation include two exemplary tomes: Stanley Elkins and Eric McKitrick, *The Age of Federalism: The Early American Republic, 1788-1800* (Oxford University Press, 1993), and the strongly anti-Hamilton and anti-Federalist book by Gordon S. Wood, *Empire of Liberty: A History of the Early Republic, 1789-1815* (Oxford University Press, 2009), in the Oxford History of the United States series. Carol Berkin, *A Sovereign People: The Crises of the 1790s and the Birth of American Nationalism* (Basic, 2017), is a welcome new addition, though it focuses on a few episodes. Other brief overviews include James Roger Sharp, *American Politics in the Early Republic: The New Nation in Crisis* (Yale University Press, 1993), and Lance Banning, *Conceived in Liberty: The Struggle to Define the New Republic, 1789-1793* (Rowman & Littlefield, 2004), in the Critical Issues in American History series.

Books on specific events of the 1790s include Fergus M. Bordewich, *The First Congress: How James Madison, George Washington, and a Group of Extraordinary Men Invented the Government* (Simon & Schuster, 2016), Harry Ammon, *The Genet Mission* (Norton, 1973), Thomas P. Slaughter, *The Whiskey Rebellion: Frontier Epilogue to the American Revolution* (Oxford University Press, 1988), Todd Estes, *The Jay Treaty Debate, Public Opinion, and the Evolution of Early American*

Political Culture (University of Massachusetts Press, 2008), Jeffrey L. Pasley, *The First Presidential Contest: 1796 and the Founding of American Democracy* (University Press of Kansas, 2013), in the American Presidential Elections series, Stephen G. Kurtz, *The Presidency of John Adams: The Collapse of Federalism, 1795-1800* (University of Pennsylvania Press, 1957), Ralph Adams Brown, *The Presidency of John Adams* (University Press of Kansas, 1970), in the American Presidency series, Alexander DeConde, *The Quasi-War: The Politics and Diplomacy of the Undeclared War with France, 1797-1801* (Scribner, 1966), Charles Slack, *Liberty's First Crisis: Adams, Jefferson, and the Misfits Who Saved Free Speech* (Grove Press, 2015), James Morton Smith, *Freedom's Fetters: The Alien and Sedition Laws and American Civil Liberties* (Cornell University Press, 1966), John Ferling, *Adams v. Jefferson: The Tumultuous Election of 1800* (Oxford University Press, 2004), in the Pivotal Moments series, and Edward J. Larson, *A Magnificent Catastrophe: The Tumultuous Election of 1800, America's First Presidential Campaign* (Free Press, 2007).

Books on the duel with Aaron Burr are also multiplying, though of dubious quality. The best place to go on the duel and dueling remains Joanne B. Freeman, *Affairs of Honor: National Politics in the New Republic* (Yale University Press, 2001), while Joseph J. Ellis raises some interesting controversial points in *Founding Brothers: The Revolutionary Generation* (Knopf, 2000). Aaron Burr is the subject of two modern biographies including David O. Stewart, *American Emperor: Aaron Burr's Challenge to Jefferson's America* (Simon & Schuster, 2011) and the revisionist Nancy Isenberg, *Fallen Founder: The Life of Aaron Burr* (Viking, 2007).

NOTES

Chapter 6

1. Ron Chernow, *Alexander Hamilton* (New York: Penguin, 2004), 154.

Chapter 7

1. Forrest McDonald, *Alexander Hamilton: A Biography* (New York: Norton, 1979), 60.

Chapter 10

1. Ron Chernow, *Alexander Hamilton* (New York: Penguin, 2004), 231–35; and Forrest McDonald, *Alexander Hamilton: A Biography* (New York: Norton, 1979), 99–105.

Chapter 11

1. Pauline Meier, *Ratification: The People Debate the Constitution, 1787-1788* (New York: Simon & Schuster, 2010), 320.

Chapter 13

1. John Lamberton Harper, *American Machiavelli: Alexander Hamilton and the Origins of American Foreign Policy* (Cambridge: Cambridge University Press, 2004), 87.

2. Thomas K. McCraw, *The Founders and Finance: How Hamilton, Gallatin, and Other Immigrants Forged a New Economy* (Cambridge: Harvard University Press, 2012), 93, 99.

3. Joseph J. Ellis, *Founding Brothers: The Revolutionary Generation* (New York: Knopf, 2000), 73.

4. Stanley Elkins and Erick McKitrick, *The Age of Federalism: The Early American Republic, 1788-1800* (Oxford: Oxford University Press, 1993), 156.

Chapter 14

1. Carson Holloway, *Hamilton versus Jefferson in the Washington Administration: Completing the Founding or Betraying the Founding?* (Cambridge: Cambridge University Press, 2015), 100.

2. Edward G. Lengl, *First Entrepreneur: How George Washington Built His—and the Nation's—Prosperity* (New York: Da Capo, 2016), 180.

Chapter 16

1. George C. Herring, *From Colony to Superpower: U.S. Foreign Relations Since 1776* (Oxford: Oxford University Press, 2008), 56.

Chapter 17

1. Thomas P. Slaughter, *The Whiskey Rebellion: Frontier Epilogue to the American Revolution* (Oxford: Oxford University Press, 1986).

2. James MacGregor Burns and Susan Dunn, *George Washington* (New York: Times Books, 2004).

Chapter 18

1. John Lamberton Harper, *American Machiavelli: Alexander Hamilton and the Origins of U.S. Foreign Policy* (Cambridge: Cambridge University Press, 2004), 130.

2. Karl-Friedrich Walling, *Republican Empire: Alexander Hamilton on War and Free Government* (Lawrence: University Press of Kansas, 1999), 211.

3. Matthew Spalding and Patrick Garrity, *A Sacred Union of Citizens: George Washington's Farewell Address and the American Character* (Lanham, MD: Rowman & Littlefield, 1996), 56.

4. Ron Chernow, *Alexander Hamilton* (New York: Penguin, 2004), 534.

Chapter 19

1. George C. Herring, *From Colony to Superpower: U.S. Foreign Relations Since 1776* (Oxford: Oxford University Press, 2008), 82.

2. Ron Chernow, *Alexander Hamilton* (New York: Penguin, 2004), 568.

Chapter 20

1. Ron Chernow, *Alexander Hamilton* (New York: Penguin, 2004), 659.

Epilogue

1. Stephen F. Knott, *Alexander Hamilton and the Persistence of Myth* (Lawrence: University Press of Kansas, 2002), and Stephen F. Knott and Tony Williams, *Washington and Hamilton: The Alliance That Forged America* (Naperville, IL: Sourcebooks, 2015).

INDEX

ABOUT THE AUTHOR

Tony Williams is a senior fellow at the Bill of Rights Institute. He earned history degrees from Syracuse University and Ohio State University. He is the coauthor of *Washington & Hamilton: The Alliance That Forged America* (with Stephen F. Knott) and several other books on the American founding. He resides in Williamsburg, Virginia, with his wife and children.